America's Home Front Heroes

America's Home Front Heroes

An Oral History of World War II

Stacy Enyeart

Foreword by Larry Aasen

PRAEGER
An Imprint of ABC-CLIO, LLC

A B C 🟡 C L I O

Santa Barbara, California • Denver, Colorado • Oxford, England

Library of Congress Cataloging-in-Publication Data

America's home front heroes: an oral history of World War II / [compiled by] Stacy Enyeart;
foreword by Larry Aasen.
     p. cm.
  Includes bibliographical references and index.
  ISBN 978-0-313-37789-1 (hard copy: acid-free paper) — ISBN 978-0-313-37790-7 (ebook)
1. World War, 1939–1945—Personal narratives, American. 2. World War,
1939–1945—United States—Biography. I. Enyeart, Stacy.
  D811.5.A18 2009
  940.53'730922—dc22   2009028495

ISBN: 978-0-313-37789-1
EISBN: 978-0-313-37790-7

13 12 11 10 09   1 2 3 4 5

This book is also available on the World Wide Web as an eBook.
Visit www.abc-clio.com for details.

Praeger
An Imprint of ABC-CLIO, LLC

ABC-CLIO, LLC
130 Cremona Drive, P.O. Box 1911
Santa Barbara, California 93116-1911

This book is printed on acid-free paper ∞

Manufactured in the United States of America

Dedicated to the wartime women pioneers in the workplace, and to their singular contribution to winning the war.

CONTENTS

Foreword by Larry Aasen   ix

Preface   xiii

Acknowledgments   xv

Introduction: Bust, Boom, and Beyond   xvii

Civilian Home Front Recollections   xxv

It Was a Time for . . . Heightened Passion   1

Civilian Survivor of Pearl Harbor Bombing—Margaret Motivalli   3

Bail or Jail—Robert Greenberg   7

Sad News from the War Department—Earl Kerker   9

Mixed Emotions during WW II—E. Harold Greist, Jr.   13

World War II through the Eyes of a Child—Charles Hazelip   16

Dear Daddy . . . From Lynette and Bud—Lynette Leynes   19

I Was a Ten-Year-Old Mascot at Panama Canal—John E. Schmidt, Jr.   21

Saying Goodbye to a Loved One—Lucille Barrett   23

Mourning the Death of a Living Soldier—Terri Webster   24

Journal Notes from a College Student—Helen Toles Buffington   26

From German Immigrant in 1927 to Doctorate in
    1956—Norman Jasper   36

Waiting for MIA News—Gordon P. Brown   39

It Was a Time for . . . Caution and Prejudice   45

A Japanese American Interned—Gene Takahashi   48

An American's Viewpoint of Internment Camps—Mary E. Williams   52

What's More Important, Pants or Your Soul?—
    Mozzelle Bearden Ivey   54

Conscientious Objector to the War—Gregg Phifer 56

Facing the War at Home as a 4-F—W.V. (Mac) McConnell 59

The Riot that Brought an Army Together—Clarence Inniss 62

It Was a Time for . . . Flag Waving 67

Wartime Housewife/Mother of Martha Stewart—Martha Kostyra 69

War Bond Tour with Jack Dempsey, Boxing Champ—Marion McManus 72

A Fighter to Be Reckoned With—Justin Barzda 75

The Corsair . . . Lean and Mean—Lee DiBattista 77

Navy WAVE Pharmacist Mate—Anne Cole-Beers 79

USO Volunteer . . . Dramatic Experiences—Vivian van Allen 82

My Postwar Experience——Del Markoff 84

Working Together in a Time of War—Mary Kowalsky 86

Key West, Florida, 1941—Armer White 89

Newspaperman in a World War II Shipyard—Frank S. Hopkins 91

It Was a Time for . . . War-Plant Women 95

Nineteen-Year-Old Depth Charge Factory Worker—Mina Burke 100

From Civilian Directly to Army WAAC—Anne Breise 102

One of the First Women Workers in the Brooklyn Navy Yard—Ida Pollack 105

From Receptionist to Payroll Unit Factory Worker—Jean Gates 107

Aiding the War Effort, as a High School Student—Josephine Maupen 110

Single in Florida . . . Date at a POW Camp—Helen Rezendes 112

A New Wave of Female Engineers—Jean Geelan 115

Reflections: Yesterday 119

Reflections: Today 121

Index 123

FOREWORD

What happened on our home front while the world watched World War II? Stacy Enyeart felt the need to share that experience with those who know little or nothing of its impact on our country's history. Using her expertise as a professional writer, television producer, and community activist for seniors, she started her journey into the past. *America's Home Front Heroes* is the result of that journey. It reveals the highly emotional time generated by the war and its effect on people back home.

This important book paints a vivid picture of on-going sacrifices on the home fronts across the United States. Luxuries were practically nonexistent and food, clothing, gasoline, and many other items were strictly rationed. New car production came to a halt. There was a ceiling price on just about everything. For those in combat each day could mean death. Those at home lived in constant fear that they would receive a dreaded telegram from the War Department. There was a daily connection, at least in spirit, between the home front and battle fronts.

Across the country, most Americans were very patriotic putting flags on their houses, collecting money for the USOs, purchasing war bonds, and making do with what they had. When the service people came home on furlough, they were treated like the heroes they were.

I saw both sides of World War II—first on the home front, then as a soldier from 1943 to 1945. As a sergeant in the glider regiment, I served in France in the 13th Airborne Division, which was one-half paratroopers and one-half glider troops. I was prepared to silently transport and drop troops across the Rhine in Germany to help General

George Patton's advance toward victory. So, from two different wartime perspectives, I submit the following.

THE HOME FRONT ON AN AMERICAN FARM

As a civilian on the home front until 1943, my life, just as everyone's, took on many new challenges but at least we were still at home in America. As a boy, growing up on a wheat farm near Fargo, North Dakota, I found that life was a constant struggle. American farms were not happy places to be during World War II. First of all, the war seemed remote to most farmers who had few if any contacts with Europe. Their machinery was old because new products were nonexistent. The country needed more food, and farmers worked double time to produce it because during the war, little or no food could be imported from abroad.

For many years before World War II, there were plenty of farm hands available to help with the harvest. During the war, most of these workers were in the army. The workers who were available were above the draft age and many were too old to be much help. More day laborers had to be found so colleges gave their students leave time to work on farms.

German prisoners of war were forced to bring in the crops. Most of these men were so happy to be out of the war that they worked hard and were well behaved and friendly. It was strange to think that only a short time before, these men—now prisoners—might have been shooting at our troops.

In *America's Home Front Heroes* we meet a few of the many women who took over wartime factory jobs when men went into the service. Well, the same routine took place down on the farm. Many housewives learned how to drive tractors, bring in the hay, and milk the cows. Although they did not look like fashion models on the tractors in all the dirt and dust and they missed their pre-war dresses, they were proud to show their husbands "that anything you can do, we can do better!"

My mother's diaries reveal some of the more subtle effects of the war on the farm home front. Two of her three sons served in France during the war. Every day she worried about them. Her good days were the days she got a letter from France. The home front story on the farm was not very pretty. It meant work from early morning to late at night. At this time our home, like many other houses, lacked electricity, central heating, and indoor plumbing. Our family's farm was near a railroad track and we would often see troop trains going by. The farmers would sometimes yell, "go kill those bastards."

THE HOME FRONT EFFECT ON SOLDIERS

In 1943 I enlisted in the army and was confronted as a soldier by the new world across the Atlantic Ocean in France. Every day soldiers thought of home and hoped for a letter. When a soldier got cheerful, happy letters from home, he knew their intent. And, when soldiers wrote home, they, too, tried to be cheerful. The death of my best friend by a landmine left behind by the Germans was an example of the kind of news that never got into letters to the home front.

The home front did a remarkable job of providing the soldiers with candy, cookies, and other welcome items. Soldiers would sometimes get their hometown newspapers. These were closely read because they wanted to know the news—both good and bad—from home, the casualties of war, those who had been discharged, and the girls who had gotten married. "Dear John" letters were often received.

To be perfectly candid, soldier's morale was crushed by news of draft dodgers, war profiteers, and photos of people living it up in the night clubs. Although most people on the home front supported the war and realized sacrifices had to be made, there were times when they, too, needed a break from the stress it caused. The familiar weekend pass served the same purpose for armed services personnel.

From my own perspective as a soldier, the home front seemed a million miles away. Although my head was on the fighting front, my heart was still at home! *America's Home Front Heroes* challenges typical history books' emphasis on facts and figures. Instead, without dismissing the harsh realities of a world at war, it highlights the human experience and brings us closer to those who went through the ordeal at home.

Sgt. Larry Aasen,
Retired U.S. Army

PREFACE

One may be prompted to ask why I was inspired to write on the overwhelming subject of the World War II home front. Frankly, it was a challenging project written to provide a nostalgic voyage for "the greatest generation," and to remind the "baby boomers" what terrific parents they have. It was also to open the eyes, minds, and hearts of today's generation by exposing them to the amazing strength and resilience of their grandparents in the face of war. Finally, it was to share a unique moment in time revealing a unified country at war to preserve peace. History will recall the home front heroes of the Second World War, but only they can verify the facts. The writing was an irresistible and rewarding experience.

America became involved in World War II in response to the Japanese bombing of our naval installations at Pearl Harbor, Hawaii, on December 7, 1941. We were blindsided by their sneak attack, which led to immediate action. That the war intimately touched the lives of innocent civilian men, women, and children worldwide is a well-known fact. More elusive today with recent generations is the impact it had on the civilian American home front.

From 1941 to 1945 each day involved a sacrifice in some way tied to helping the war effort. Luxuries were a thing of the past. Just imagine in the "land of plenty," food, clothing, and gasoline being strictly rationed, new car production coming to a halt, and a sudden and serious lifestyle change for all! The O.P.A. (Office of Price Administration) was created to put a ceiling price on just about everything. Did we complain? Absolutely! Grumbling was rampant, but patriotism was flying high so we adjusted to the imposed regulation. Unfortunately, we must make note of those who took advantage of these tough times and showed a disregard for patriotism. When the O.P.A. was created, money-hungry individuals operated "black markets" for those who could afford their excessive prices for goods.

America's Home Front Heroes is an uncomplicated look at the complex American home front. It is not focused on dates that we tend to forget or details typically offered by historians; instead, it highlights the civilian impact and mood of an emotionally charged era. It was shake-up time for American traditions, including the conventional female role of the housewife, shifting her into the wartime workplace outside the home. It spawned an unprecedented period of America's growth and prosperity. It left in its wake a self-sacrificing generation of young people; some of whom, sixty-three years later, have chosen to share through letters, journals, and interviews their recollections and often bittersweet experiences, painting an eyewitness portrait during a war-time home front. It is important to look back and reflect on the home front as we survived its trials and tribulations. I can't help thinking how fortunate we are to have this valuable resource as an example from which to draw strength and resilience today.

The World War II home front as a subject has intrigued this author for decades. It has been the focus of writers and film makers over the years, but few from the generation who lived through the era. In reading their personal submissions, a feeling of kinship with each participant and an obligation to share these collective experiences became my contribution. It became even more important to me as the passage of time will soon silence the voices of those who lived the experience, leaving history books as the only source of reference.

ACKNOWLEDGMENTS

It is with endless appreciation that I acknowledge those men and women who made possible the writing of this book—namely the home front heroes of World War II and their personal sacrifices. To complete the picture, my thanks for the help and support of those mentioned below and their steadfast belief in the project. Their names are presented in no particular order of recognition.

To Joanne Dearcopp—For her patience; firm, soft-spoken advice; her clear concept of the book's content and her valuable consultation.

To Dr. David Harper, D. Min—Over a long journey of writing, his spiritual and pragmatic counsel were inspiring. His ability to relate to the subject matter and empathize with the task at hand was a constant source of encouragement.

To the Westport Public Library reference department staff—For those who always provided the urgently needed answers to questions. And, of course, to the library as an amazing research source.

To Teresa Errico and Neal Casaubon—Local college students, who served as editorial assistants and grew to understand the significance of the World War II home front, a subject rather unfamiliar to them and apparently many other young students.

To my Pen Women pals (National League of American Pen Women)—For those who served, sometimes unknowingly, as a support group of creative women.

To Florida State University, Institute on World War II and the Human Experience—for the wealth of their resources.

And last, but not least, to a variety of other people who kept me on track with their positive reaction to the book's concept.

INTRODUCTION: BUST, BOOM, AND BEYOND

It is said history repeats itself; with good reason, it is the ultimate teacher. Using history as a barometer we can learn from our mistakes as well as victories, and stay ahead of the game. With this assumption we travel back in our country's history to the year 1939.

Although America had been sending "Bundles for Britain" (food, clothing, and other civilian necessities) and war materiel since 1939 to help stem the German advance, Britain was being overwhelmed. Hitler's fire of invasion and inhumane atrocities were sweeping across Europe killing thousands and destroying cities and irreplaceable landmarks. Our isolationist policy and the great Atlantic Ocean gave the United States a sense of security against attack, so we still hesitated to get involved. Our official position was "hands off," allowing Great Britain, Russia, and allies to defend their respective borders.

Despite maintaining neutrality, when Germany invaded France in May 1940 and took control of Paris, we saw the handwriting on the wall and began drafting young men 25 to 35 years of age into military service.

Unfortunately, we had just emerged from the Great Depression of the 1930s, where fortunes were lost overnight in a collapsed stock market. Bread lines and soup kitchens were common, as rich and poor alike shared in the economic debacle. Then came help. In early 1941, thousands of new jobs were suddenly created with the enactment of the Lend-Lease Act. This two-fold bill allowed us to increase production of military armament; sell weapons, food, and equipment to the desperate war-torn European community; and at the same time helped strengthen our own neglected military establishment. With the bombing of

Pearl Harbor in 1941, the U.S. Congress declared war on Japan and Germany and to shore up our much-needed manpower reserve 18- to 45-year-old men were eligible for the "draft." Now, all-too-soon, we were coping with another disaster—out of the Depression and into a two-front global conflict. Our priorities and life in America changed drastically as the home front geared up for a long struggle.

> . . . So this is war. This hustle-bustle, hurrying world we live in today. Seems like everything is speeded up and, of course, it is. It has to be so we can win this war. I am an American, an American who is experiencing war for the first time. This war is making us of the younger generation grow old fast, and who can help it? We have watched the happy-go-lucky America of peace time plunge whole-heartedly into winning the war. At my school the next day, everyone was excited. 'What would happen now?' we asked. I think most of us expected the Japs to march into New York any minute. That's how little we knew of war.
> —Helen Toles Buffington, GA, 1999, WWII Memories

There was a dark side to life on the home front. There were black markets for almost everything; for a price one could find nylons, sugar, butter, cigarettes, and gasoline. Illegal profiteering grew, and when caught, participants were subject to severe consequences. Fortunately most Americans were loyal to the cause. It was hard to believe that the simple staples of life were virtually legally unavailable to everyone except through their ration books.

We were on heightened alert, and warned that saboteurs and spies had been brought in to Long Island, New York, under the cover of darkness. There was speculation that German U-boats could be in the Long Island Sound. Where was the great Atlantic Ocean barrier we had relied on for so long? Some civilians scanned the night skies for enemy aircraft and patrolled familiar neighborhoods searching for tiny specks of light coming from behind carelessly closed window curtains. A total blackout was enforced, and even vehicle headlights were partially painted over.

As a senior in high school, I was old enough to be an Assistant Air Raid
Warden. If we saw any, even a spec of light, we had to knock on their
door and make them black out their windows better in case of enemy air
attack. If anyone was out walking they could not carry a flash light either.
—Mary Kowalsky, CT, April 2001, WWII Memories

As the war continued there were shortages of everything, everywhere. The home front was a paradox . . . sad, joyful, colorful, mono-
tone, patriotic, greedy, cooperative, riotous, depressing, and euphoric.
Single women, housewives, and men who were too old or physically
unable to serve on the battlefield manned the home front. Military
deferments were judiciously given to some factory management workers, engineers designing our war machines, students about to graduate,
or young men whose families were dependent on them for financial
support.

Of all the shortages, perhaps the most contentious was gasoline
rationing. Depending on need, A, B, or C gasoline stickers were issued
for car windshields, C being the most coveted as it allowed for more
buying power. A full tank of gas was out of the question, a quarter of a
tank was the norm, and pleasure driving was impossible.

*Five college boys at the University of Florida car pooled back home to see
their folks. They ran out of gas, found a small filling station and country
store where the owner lived on premises.*
They were closed so we blew our car horn, nothing happened. We
walked around, found an unlocked KEROSENE pump, left some money,
put a couple of gallons in to our old Model A and drove off. That good
old car would run on ANYTHING.
—Robert Greenberg, FL, 1998, WWII Memories

Trolley tracks were uprooted everywhere for re-smelting, as heavy
structural steel was needed and everything was sacrificed for the war
effort. Any taken-for-granted item was in very short supply. Rents were
high, inflation was rampant . . . life was not a bed of roses. However,
there was a sense of euphoria for those untouched by personal loss, and
enjoying the economic upturn due to an increase in job opportunities.

In March 1945 a father wrote to his son in the Navy.
The automobile is still running good, and I still have the pre-war tires
and not in bad shape. There are no new cars being made. Some foods
also, like meat, are off the market at times, however we eat enough so
don't worry. There should be plenty of work after the war as no repair
or replacement work has been done for years.
—Douglas Leach, TN, 2000, WWII Memories

The familiar poster of Rosie the Riveter became the symbol for
women working with great pride in unfamiliar war factory environ-
ments building aircraft; making bomb components, parachutes, nuts
and bolts; and in the process breaking fingernails and getting greasy for
the cause. Although the character Rosie was fictional, born out of a
song title, the image was powerful and she became a role model for
thousands of women!

Thousands of V-Mail (V for Victory) letters were written to bolster
spirits in the Armed Forces. These were lightweight form letters which
were photographed and the film was flown overseas and reproduced at
mail centers around the world, thereby reducing the time it took to get
to loved ones.

The United Service Organizations (which quickly became known as
the USO) played a big role in helping the war effort. President Roosevelt asked the Young Men's Christian Association, National Catholic
Community Service, the National Traders Aid Association, the
National Jewish Welfare Aid Association, and the Salvation Army to
handle the on-leave entertainment of the armed forces. The five organ-
izational resources were incorporated as the USO in New York State as
a private nonprofit organization in February 1942. At its high point in
1949, USOs were found in over 3,000 locations throughout the United
States.

Comedian Bob Hope made his first USO tour in 1942 and continued
to do so for more than five decades. An off-shoot of the USO was The
Stage Door Canteen, a nightclub for servicemen in New York City,
where the troops were entertained by top performers. The movie and
music industry played its part on the home front. Big dance bands
reflected on every aspect of the war. Songs like "Soldier Let me Read
Your Letter," "Don't Sit under the Apple Tree," "I'll Be Seeing You,"

and many others brought tears to the eyes of millions who waited and prayed for the day when the world would be free and their men would return home. Movies like *Since You Went Away* starring Fredric March and Myrna Loy; *Stage Door Canteen* featuring Tallulah Bankhead, Katharine Hepburn, and many big bands of the era; and *The Clock* with Judy Garland and Robert Walker depicted the lives of servicemen on leave in the big city. These movies were big hits and for a few hours in the darkened theater made us feel closer to loved ones overseas.

BOOM TIME

As if to soften the blow of a long struggle, America's post-World War II economic rebound was unequalled to date. It was appropriately called a "boom time," releasing the pent-up frustration of a nation on a strict wartime diet and now ready for a huge meal! After four long years of conflict, Americans were bursting for a come-back to the norm. All national resources, creativity, and willpower were set in motion and focused on building an even stronger, peace-loving America.

The immediate post-war period could be referred to as "the good times," with Americans riding high on a booming economy bubbling with new products for thirsty consumers.

> My life was great. How lucky I was! At the same time for so many others new opportunities presented themselves, that because of World War II and its aftermath simply could not have existed pre-war. Yes, it was a great time in my life. But it was also a great time for my country. How fortunate to have been an American at that time. I smile every time I think of the halcyon days of 1945 to 1949!
> —Del Markoff, CT, April 2002, WWII Memories

In 1946 factories returned to building Buicks instead of bombs, and servicemen and women moth-balled their uniforms and donned "civvies." New roads and bridges were constructed to accommodate travelers and commerce. Movie stars like Clark Gable, James Stewart, Henry Fonda, who had been called into service, returned to the big screen and they were welcomed back to one of the great American pastimes. Major League baseball icons like Ted Williams and Joe DiMaggio were also back on the scene along with other professional sports figures. New homes, new everything from marriages to baby carriages were in evidence, and Americans bought it all! An economic explosion was underway that would begin another chapter in America's history. Improvements to our way of life were made on almost every front, and as a result provided job opportunities in unprecedented numbers.

The Marshall Plan bore much of the responsibility for the economic upturn. It encouraged European nations to work together for economic recovery after World War II. In June 1947, the United States agreed to administer aid to Europe if the countries would meet to decide what they needed. The official name of the plan was the European Recovery Program; however, it is called the Marshall Plan because the Secretary of State, George C. Marshall initiated the concept. It became active in April 1946 when Congress established the Economic Cooperation Administration (ECA) to administer foreign aid. Seventeen nations formed the Organization for European Economic Cooperation (OEEC) to assist the ECA. Until 1952, the United States sent about $13 billion in food, machinery, and other products to Europe.

RETROSPECTIVE

The present-day battle with radical Islam occurred when, for the second time in history, America was viciously and unexpectedly attacked from the air on September 11, 2001. The initial blow took place at 8:46 A.M. as the work force in a busy office complex took their places in the target zone, unaware of their fate. The 110-story World Trade Center Towers in New York City were totally destroyed. Two hundred forty miles away in Washington, D.C., a large section of the United States Pentagon, filled with personnel, was severely damaged. Simultaneously, another commercial aircraft, United Airlines flight 93, with approximately forty passengers and crew aboard was hijacked, with the White House as the target for destruction. Against the odds, a desperate attempt to gain control over the terrorists failed, and the heroic passengers went down in a field in Pennsylvania, killing all aboard. Horror and disbelief at these four coordinated attacks were widespread throughout the civilized world.

America's Home Front Heroes speaks from the author's perspective as a witness to the war years that now, sixty-four years later, are referenced almost daily in the media. Although United States soil was left unscathed by enemy destruction during World War II (Hawaii was not yet a state), the war mongers and battle fronts were clearly defined.

Such is not the case in today's war on terror, which knows no boundaries and every stone must be overturned to reveal the enemy. As part of the counter-terrorism effort, perhaps a government-sponsored civilian volunteer program could become the link between our mission and a united home front, to be labeled the civilian counterattack!

This book highlights recollections from some who were there during those dark days of World War II. The war's long-term impact on many is indisputable. There are no fictional characters or situations in this book . . . just people from all walks of life, with one thing in common . . . a shared experience in another battle of sorts on the home front.

Their contributions continue to stand as a testament to the enduring American spirit.

My family all worked for the war. My father (who had an eighth grade education) taught mechanics at a local high school. My mother took a Red Cross class and worked at the local hospital. My older sister worked in a defense plant in Southern Indiana, and my younger sister joined the Cadet Nurse Corps in Gary, Indiana.
—Mina Burke, IN, April 1999, WWII Memories

A salute and never-ending gratitude to the American armed forces, who fought and died so valiantly in World War II to preserve the freedoms we cherish. During war time the ultimate sacrifice is the life of a loved one. In more than four years of war, from 1941 to 1945, on the ground, in the air, and on the sea, 405,399 American service men and women paid with their lives in the European and Pacific theaters—an unforgettable contribution to the free world.

On June 22, 1944 President Franklin D. Roosevelt signed the G.I. Bill of Rights as enacted by the Congress of The United States. The Bill was officially known as the Serviceman's Readjustment Act and was designed to provide greater opportunities to returning war veterans, such as aid in adjusting to civilian life, in the areas of hospitalization, the purchase of homes and businesses, and especially education. This Act provided tuition, subsistence, books, and supplies, equipment and counseling services to enable veterans to continue their education in high school or college.

Approximately one year after signing the G.I. Bill of Rights a series of events occurred with major consequences. On April 12 of 1945 just prior to the war's end, President Roosevelt died suddenly and for many days the nation mourned his passing. He had been in office as president for an unprecedented four terms, and was a familiar figure to all. Vice President Harry S. Truman was immediately sworn into office as President of the United States. It was upon his decision that two very controversial and powerful weapons of war called atomic bombs were dropped on the cities of Hiroshima (August 6, 1945) and Nagasaki (August 9, 1945) thereby ending World War II. War with Germany had ended several months earlier, on May 7, 1945 at Allied Headquarters in Remis, France with an unconditional surrender! The Japanese surrendered on September 2, 1945 in a ceremony aboard the USS *Missouri* in Tokyo Bay.

Was the cause worth the fight? Consider the alternative.

CIVILIAN HOME FRONT RECOLLECTIONS

The following stories represent only one drop in a sea of experiences on the World War II home front. How each reader benefits from these revelations depends on his or her willingness to listen and learn from these proud Americans. Hopefully, they will contribute to an understanding of the difference in sacrifice between home front generations of yesterday and today, and realize that the character of a free nation is determined by its citizens. They are the glue that through team effort holds America together.

A wartime home front should be demanding of personal time, energy, skills, and daily sacrifice; otherwise, there is a disconnect between the outfield and home plate. In disagreement with this philosophy, one might call it a "two-generational" gap attitude. Perhaps more appropriate with today's different kind of war scenario, we can refer to the lack of civilian involvement as a "responsibility" gap. Nationwide, during World War II Americans contributed to winning the war in a very personal way. Writing this book and highlighting their recollections is the author's belated contribution.

So, remember America's home front heroes of World War II . . . one may belong to you.

Part I

It Was a Time for ...
Heightened Passion

WESTERN UNION

1201

A. N. WILLIAMS
PRESIDENT

The filing time shown in the date line on telegrams and day letters is STANDARD TIME at point of origin. Time of receipt is STANDARD TIME at point of destination

ST6 53 GOVT=WUX WASHINGTON DC APR 25 457P

MRS GUYTHA S WEBSTER=240 PROVINCE ST RICHFORD VT=

I AM PLEASED TO INFORM YOU THAT A CORRECTED REPORT HAS BEEN
ECEIVED FROM THE THEATER OF OPERATIONS WHICH STATES THAT YOUR
SON PRIVATE FIRST CLASS DONALD W WEBSTER HAS BEEN RELEASED FROM
GERMAN HOSPITAL AND WAS NOT REPEAT NOT KILLED IN ACTION 26
DECEMBER AS YOU WERE PREVIOUSLY INFORMED LETTER FOLLOWS=

:J A ULIO THE ADJUTANT GENERAL. 515P....

Courtesy Terri Webster

Without the benefit of personal experience, few can appreciate the devastating, relentless anxiety on the home front while living through a full-blown war. We all knew someone who was serving in the military, and that just heightened the pressure. Life took on a new focus in all directions.

Tears, joy, sentimentality, and hope were all possible reactions at any given moment. It was an emotional roller-coaster ride, depending on events as they unfolded from day to day: a serviceman lost, found, wounded, or sending a V-mail letter of encouragement to folks at home. For many families, it meant coping alone with life's inevitable problems minus the love and valuable support of a partner.

Civilian Survivor of Pearl Harbor Bombing

Margaret Motivalli, Connecticut

Do I remember Pearl Harbor? You bet. I was there when the bombs first started dropping at 8 A.M. Sunday, December 7, 1941. I was 12 years old and the memory is etched in my mind. My father was stationed at the Hickham Field Army Air Force Base on the island of Oahu that fateful day. He was a Signal Corps officer and graduate of West Point; in fact, I was born in West Point, New York. A few years later Hawaii became our home for a total of seven happy years, but that happiness was destroyed by the Japanese Imperial Air Force attack.

At first we saw smoke coming from the huge oil tanks reserve at Pearl Harbor and thought they had been sabotaged. Then my dad spotted enemy aircraft and we were in trouble! He had to immediately report for duty leaving my mother, myself, and three siblings home alone! Shrapnel from our anti-aircraft guns was falling all around our house, people were running everywhere . . . it was sheer panic. Our house was located in view of the harbor entrance where so many battleships were moored. I ran out of the house looking for our dog, and a Japanese fighter pilot flew so low over the house I could actually see his face!

An Air Force officer in our neighborhood came by looking very distraught, and reported that a barracks housing 2,000 men had taken a direct hit. My little family was fortunate to be alive. We gathered together a few items and immediately drove to Honolulu, where my mother's sister was living. When we told them of the attack on Pearl Harbor, they thought at first we were kidding. Sadly, we were not! As if we were not stressed enough, for a week we did not know the state of my dad. We learned he came through the terror okay, much to our relief.

It took several months, but all American dependents were ordered home by the U.S. government. San Francisco was our destination, aboard the luxury liner *Lurline* of the Matson line. It was very over-crowded with mostly women and children. It required several sittings at mealtime, and ten days surrounded by a convoy of four or five ships, escorted by a Navy destroyer to reach port in San Francisco. Midway, one of the ships had to stop for repairs, which made us twenty-four hours late in crossing, but probably saved our lives as we learned a Japanese submarine had been laying in wait for us, and had finally given up and left the area.

We disembarked in San Francisco and stayed for about six weeks because we had only warm weather clothing, then took a four-day train trip across the country. We made our way to Boston, Massachusetts, in route to my grandfather's house in Waltham, Massachusetts. In the meantime, my dad remained in Hawaii, and sometime later was assigned to Guadalcanal with the Marine Corps. He was stationed there for two years until he contracted malaria, and was then shipped home in 1943 and assigned to duty at Fort Monmouth, New Jersey. We packed up and moved from Massachusetts to be with him. The war came to an end in 1945.

No doubt, my life was forever changed because of Pearl Harbor. For many years after our experience there, it was never a topic of conversation in our family. To a young 12-year-old girl, the island of Oahu was a paradise. I loved my life there and to see it destroyed was unforgettable. All this took place many, many years ago and some of my memories may be a bit rusty, but you can be sure of its impact on me. To this day, in this regard, I never truly feel a sense of security.

As a final ironic note, immediately following the terrorist attack in New York City on September 11, 2001, I decided to drive to the home of my son living in Fairfield, Connecticut. As I walked to my car, a plane flew overhead in the "no-fly zone" enforced by the government, and I was reminded of another similar incident sixty years earlier! Before reaching my son's home I stopped for a moment and looked back, saw smoke in the distance coming from the Twin Towers' explosion in New York City and was once again reminded of December 7, 1941 . . . an amazing parallel. I realize just how fragile our lives can be in this uncertain world!

Signal Corps Officer Maurice Motivalli stationed at Hickham Field Air Force Base on the island of Oahu, Hawaii [Courtesy Margaret Motivalli]

Margaret Motivalli, age 12, was witness to the Japanese bombing of Pearl Harbor on December 7, 1941. [Courtesy Margaret Motivalli]

Bail or Jail

Robert Greenberg, Florida

The year was 1941. WWII was raging. There were five of us, driving home for the weekend. We were sophomores at the University of Florida and carpooled back to Tallahassee to visit our families. Sharing rides was necessary because of gas rationing and, luckily, we managed to scrounge up enough ration stamps to fill the tank whenever we found a station.

On Sunday afternoon we started back to Gainesville. We were low on gas when we started out and figured we would fill up once we reached Perry. When we arrived, we were dismayed to see everything was closed up. With a little left, we said, "We'll go on to Mayo."

We get to Mayo and there is nothing. The man at the bus station said that up the road about a mile or two was a small filling station and a country store. We were informed the man who owned it lives in the back. If we went up there and woke him up, he might sell us some gas. The five of us were desperate to get back. We had classes and ROTC the next day.

It was dark when we parked in front of the station. We knocked on the door, blew on the horn. Nothing happened. My roommate and I said, "We'll go around back and see if we can wake him up." We beat on the door, but after a period of time, realized it was hopeless. We walked back to the front only to find out that our friends had discovered an unlocked kerosene pump. They put a couple of gallons into the old Model A. That car would run on anything.

We took the gas and responsibly left some money and stamps in return. Times were tough and we barely had any money, but we pooled a collection together. Our plan was to leave it on the owner's car, which was parked out back. Just as we walked over to drop off the money, the lights came on. Out walks a double-barrel shotgun with a little man behind it demanding, "Stop right there. I've already called the sheriff." We tried to explain what was going on, but our efforts were in vain. He would not listen.

The sheriff came and escorted us back to Live Oak—the Suwanee County Jail—where we spent the night imprisoned. The jail at this time consisted of a corridor down the middle with cells on both side. Each cell had a door that was completely solid except for a window at the top and a little slot at the bottom through which they could pass food. My roommate and I were in one cell and the other guys were across the hall. On our side, the windows were closed. On their side, the windows were open for some reason, and it was cold.

In the cell next to mine I could not see through the wall. My neighbors could see through their little peephole, though. Imprisoned beside me was a Black woman who was an escapee from Chattahoochee. They had caught her and were holding her until the people from Chattahoochee could come get her. She heard us out there and she entertained us all night with some of the wildest babblings I had ever heard. The woman was delusional and scatological in her conversation. At one point, our driving companions across the hall were looking out and she either turned the water on or stopped up the commode. Water began to pour out of her cell. Luckily for my roommate and I, it only flowed across the hall. Here were these poor guys standing with their feet soaking wet and freezing air blowing through their window.

The next morning the sheriff said that we had to post bond. We had no money and I did not want to have to call my parents and tell them I was in jail. Finally, I remembered I knew someone in town who was a friend of my father's. I figured I could go ask him to lend me the money without telling my folks. We could get away with it. The sheriff released my roommate and I to see if we could raise the bond.

On our way to find this man, my roommate finally confessed and said he had a savings account in Milton with enough money in it for bail. I insisted that we call his bank and were successful in withdrawing the money. We paid the bond.

One of the perpetrators on our trip happened to be the son of the dean of Florida State University. He phoned his father to tell him what had occurred. The dean, in turn, went and spoke with the governor about the incident. In the end, the sheriff who arrested us was removed from office. Our police records were cleared, we were given our money back, and all was well.

Sad News from the War Department

Earl Kerker, Illinois

Perhaps the hardest part of being on the home front was receiving the news about the death of a family member. Barton Kerker was killed in Italy when his plane crashed into a mountain returning from a bombing mission. The family received many letters of condolences and offers of assistance from official and unofficial sources. The following were sent to his mother and father.

FIFTEENTH AIR FORCE
Office of the Commanding General
A. P. O. 520

13 January 1945

Mr. Fay H. Kerker
Nemaha, Nebraska

Dear Mr. Kerker:

I am very sorry that I must confirm the report of the War
Department that your son, Flight Officer Barton G. Kerker,
T-5656, passed away on December 20, 1944, while returning
from a combat mission. The crew thought that they had
sufficient altitude to pass over any obstacles which might
be encountered on the return flight through dense clouds.
I regret that I must report that the ship crashed into a
mountain peak, killing the entire crew at once. Barton
was given a military funeral and rests in an American
cemetery in Italy, the exact location of which will be
made known to you when security regulations permit.

Your son's personal possessions have been assembled for
shipment to the Effects Quartermaster, Army Effects Bureau,
Kansas City, Missouri, who will in turn forward them to the
designated beneficiary.

During his career with this air force your son made an im-
measurable contribution to the struggle that engages us.
Barton won the respect and admiration of all his associates
for the many sterling traits of character which he posses-
sed. In the name of a grateful nation and in behalf of
the many comrades here who miss your son keenly, I extend
heartfelt sympathy.

Very sincerely yours,

N. F. TWINING
Major General, USA
Commanding

Courtesy Earl Kerker

Flight Officer Barton C. Kerker [Courtesy Earl Kerker]

Barton Kerker's final resting place at the American Cemetery in Florence, Italy. [Courtesy Earl Kerker]

Mixed Emotions during WWII

E. Harold Greist, Jr., Connecticut

In late 1941, I was an 18-year-old student who had dropped out of college almost a year earlier to earn money to continue pursuing an engineering degree. I was working in a lab, having started at minimum hourly wage of 40 cents, then proudly advanced to 45, and finally, 50 cents an hour. Twenty dollars for a 40-hour work week! It was not enough to afford a new $1,600 Chrysler or even $700 for a new Ford V8, but it was enough to buy my first car for $85. It was a used 1936 Hudson Terraplane and I fed it with regular gas at 17 cents a gallon.

My parents, bless them, continued to provide my room and board for free, so I could save for college and even take my fiancée out dancing the Lindy to big swing music on Saturday nights. My direct supervisor's $35 per week enabled him to support his wife and their two children.

Although we were quite aware of and concerned about the Nazi attacks on Europe, most of us 132+ million Americans (1940 census count) felt safe and pursued our normal peacetime lives. Then December 7th happened and abruptly changed *everything*. America was the object of a surprise attack by Japan and subsequent declaration of war by Germany. The personal priorities of most Americans were swiftly transformed. Thousands volunteered for military service despite compensation as little as "$21 for a day—once a month!" as described in a then-popular song. The hearts and minds of millions of Americans fused them into a powerful force with a single objective—*to save democracy from tyranny*. And so the "Greatest Generation" came into being.

I wanted to volunteer for pilot training and hoped my dad would approve. I always looked up to my dad. He was a tremendous role model and a real hero. He had fought for our country, first in the U.S. Cavalry on the Mexican border, and then in World War I as an Army pilot and Flight Commander in the Signal Corps' 90th Aero Squadron.

(The 90th still exists as part of today's U.S. Air Force.) Less than 400 Americans actually flew into combat during WWI, in planes made of wood and lacquered fabric, but no body-armor. Fliers had no parachutes, because the first practical chutes weren't available until just before the end of the war. Dad had been awarded a citation for "extraordinary heroism in combat with an armed enemy of the United States" that was personally presented by none other than the renowned four-star commanding General John J. Pershing.

Asking Dad's approval, I said, "Now it's *my* turn to follow your lead by volunteering for active service in the Army Air Force right now—okay with you?" He replied, "I like your resolve, but I question your timing. I know you already have received some ROTC training in prep school and college, but are you really in shape mentally and physically to give your country your *very* best? Right now all you can offer is a body that's in mediocre condition without a chance to recover from late social nights . . . and a brain that has so far completed only one semester of college. . . . "So my advice, Son, is this: Apply for Air Cadet training in the Reserve forces and let them decide when to call you into active duty. Meanwhile, continue your education and get your body into better shape." I followed his advice, returned to college and joined the Reserves.

America's home front buckled down to the serious business of supporting our own war effort and those of our allies. Indeed, in his special broadcast on December 29, 1940, our President Franklin Roosevelt declared, "We must become an Arsenal of Democracy," a term that captured the hearts and will of all Americans.

The national speed limit became 35 miles per hour, and those who chose to drive at higher speeds, wasting precious gasoline needed for our war effort, were scorned as un-American. Gas was rationed and so was meat and sugar. Lucky Strike cigarette ads proclaimed, "LS green goes to war." The green packaging color was removed to conserve a scarce ingredient used in marking green ink that was "critically needed" (a new expression connoting urgency). "For the war effort" conveyed priority status.

Private powerboats of 100+ feet in length were requisitioned from private owners for the Offshore Yacht Patrol crewed by Navy personnel. The Patrol existed until enough of the swift sub-chasers were built to take over coastline search missions for enemy submarines that might otherwise deposit enemy frogmen on our shores. The transformation of each private yacht included fore-and-aft instillation of machine gun mounts. Dispossessed yacht owners cringed at the realization that their gleaming brass fixtures, which cost them a small fortune, would meet the same depressing fate as their precious panels of glowing mahogany and teakwood. Each would receive a generous coating of no-nonsense navy gray paint. Lay it on thick, Sailor!

By age 19, having completed almost three college semesters since Pearl Harbor, I received orders to report for active duty, starting with basic training, then classification as a pilot, a bombardier, or a navigator. I was selected for pilot training. By age 20, I had been promoted to Captain in command of a squadron of 240 cadets in the Southeastern Training Command. I was thrilled and thought it was because of my training at Staunton Military Academy and college ROTC. My sister said it was simply because I had a loud enough voice to make it easy for my men to hear my commands.

Soon after I was called to active duty, my fiancée joined the Navy WAVES. She later met a nice guy and gave back the engagement ring I had given to her. Do girls love sailors best?

The War was still on when my dream of following my father's footsteps was cut short and I received medical discharge due to a service-connected physical disability. Although some friends said I was lucky to be out, I was disappointed and, given the chance, would have rejoined in a heartbeat! At least I could still wear my "ruptured duck," a small gold badge to be worn on a civilian lapel to indicate a veteran with a medical discharge.

After discharge and before completing my undergraduate work, I resumed a role in the home front support, working as a Suggestion Investigator in a GE division that made precision turret motors for American warplanes. During World War II, individual Americans paid whatever they could—their work, their love, and those heroes among us even gave their limbs or their lives.

World War II through the Eyes of a Child

Charles Hazelip, Florida

I was born in Baltimore, Maryland, in 1933, so I was only 6 years of age when the German army marched into Poland. I had no idea about what was going on. Life seemed to be pretty slow and sunny, as I recall. I was 8 years of age when all my family (four older sisters and Mom and Dad) was gathered in the living room on a Sunday in December. They were listening to a report about how "the Japs" had bombed Pearl Harbor in Honolulu, Hawaii. I had no idea where that was, and I wasn't sure who "the Japs" were. Soon, President Roosevelt, the only president of the USA that I knew throughout my entire lifetime up to that point, came on the radio and said our country was going to fight "the Japs" because they had pulled a dirty sneak attack on our navy at Pearl Harbor and killed a lot of our sailors and sank many of our battleships.

Soon after that day I learned that we were also going to fight the Germans because some funny-looking man with a black toothbrush moustache was beating up all the countries in Europe, which I believed to be the rest of the world. I began to see pictures of war planes, submarines, tanks, machine guns, and soldiers equipped with all sorts of guns. I was hooked. As a child, I loved it.

At the post offices of that time you could get large white posters that depicted the silhouettes of both allied and axis war planes. We were encouraged to study these posters so that we could spot enemy aircraft by the shape of their silhouettes and report the spotting to someone, I wasn't sure who. I studied diligently. Soon I could identify the German Stuka dive bomber, the Me 109 fighter, the Henkel 110, light bomber, the Japanese Zero, English Spitfires, Hawker Hurricanes, our own P-38, Thunderbird, Grumman Wildcat, Sikorsky Corsair, and a host of others, now lost to memory over 50-plus years. Then, however, I was ready. Daily I searched the skies for the first sighting of the enemy. To top it off, my dad volunteered to look for German submarines in the Chesapeake Bay from his fishing boat, while fishing, of course. Dad was a little grumpy about this war. I had heard him say with some disgust that he was "too young for the first one and too old for this one!" This made him angry.

As I mentioned, I had four older sisters. By the time I was 9 years old, they were regulars at a place called the USO. All I knew about it was that they went there to dance with soldiers and sailors. It seemed to me that all young men were either a sailor or marine, except for one guy my oldest sister was going with who was not able to be because of a serious childhood illness. He was a machinist who was working in a factory where they made parts of war machines. The three other girls brought crowds of servicemen home with them from the USO to continue dancing in the basement of our house. My dad got an old Wurlitzer juke box from somewhere, rigged it so you wouldn't have to put in money, and the girls and these service guys would dance for hours down in the basement. I watched from the stairs. One time we had a flooded basement because of heavy rain. That did not stop the dancing, however. I remember watching servicemen, enlisted, officer, soldier, sailor, marine, it didn't matter, with their trousers rolled up swabbing the basement floor so they could turn on the juke box and get to dancing.

Some of these men I never saw again, I don't know what became of them. Three of them married my three youngest sisters. My oldest sister married the man who worked in the defense plant. At the age of 10 or 11 I still saw only the excitement of the war, without realizing the danger and heartbreak that was associated with combat. One night my mom, dad, and sister Norma went to the movies. The picture was *Sands of Iwo Jima*. After the show we were walking up the street when Norma burst into tears. She was frightened by the movies because she could picture her boyfriend, Ron Schoelkopf, in the same terrible combat shown in the movie. As a typical boy of 10, I couldn't see why she was concerned, because Ron was fighting the Germans, not "the Japs" like John Wayne was in the movies.

As I approached 12 or 13 years of age, I began receiving through the mail items of enemy equipment. Ron was sending me souvenirs from his service in Germany. I received a German officer's uniform, a bayonet, and (piece by piece) a 9-mm Mauser rifle. As I look back on his actions in sending these items I marvel at what he was doing. Then, I did not appreciate these items for what they were and, except for the rifle, I traded them away to friends who were much smarter than I and who knew what it would mean to have the items in the future.

Wartime in Baltimore meant "black outs." At various times, at a given signal, all lights in the city were to be turned off. It was an eerie sight to see all the lights in the neighborhood go off at one time, not by a power outage, but to keep the enemy bombers from finding their target. Block wardens roamed the streets in the dark admonishing any careless person who left a light on, or who even lit a cigarette. Nobody wanted to get called down for giving the enemy a target to bomb.

In many windows there hung small red, white, and blue flags. Not American flags, but little banners of the same colors. In the white fields of these banners there would appear one, two, or even more blue stars. One star for each service member from that house. The Wissmens, old family friends, had three blue stars on their banner. One day when I went to their house to pick up something for my mom I noticed that there was now one gold star and two blue stars on the banner. I later found out that the gold star was for their eldest son who was blown out of the turret of his tank in North Africa. I believe I began to understand that there were real human effects that came from a war at that point. Their son was a good friend to my family and we would never see him again. His mom, a usually happy, outgoing person, seemed sadder forever after.

I was 12 in 1945, and the war was ending. FDR died and I then realized that someone else was going to be president. When President Truman let us drop "The Bomb," I was as awestruck as anyone else by the destruction and killing it caused. For me, war then became something other than glamorous. I cannot deny that the attraction of war captured me, and probably led to my choice of a career in the military. I know now that war—any war—is a dirty, deceptive, clumsy, awful way to accomplish anything. As a people we need to rise above it, but whether or not we can do so is a question for the ages.

Dear Daddy ... From Lynette and Bud

Lynette Leynes, Florida

Bernhardt Leynes joined the Navy in Jacksonville, Florida in 1943. He was assigned to a CB Battalion and served in Africa, Italy, and France. The following letters are from his children to him during the war.

813 East Call Street
Tallahassee, Florida
February 2?, 1944

Dear Daddy,

How are you? I hope very much that you are well.

Daddy, thank you very much for the pin, candy, and everything else you sent us. I have had so many complements on my pin.

Saturday mother bought me eight records as Evelyn Blackburn said she would let us use her victrola. The names of the records are as follows: String of Pearls, Yes Indeed!, Oh! Lady be Good, Stompin' at the Savoy, Song of India, Begin the Beguine, Don't be that Way, and I can't think of the other one.

Thursday we had a math test and I made 100%. Annie Merle made 94%.

We are working on a new piece of music in band named "Symphony in F Minor No. 4". It really is hard, mostly mine.

I paid for two pictures of band. I will send them both to you & let you select the one you want.

Evelyn Hemmingway saw her daddy Sunday night for the first time in two years. He is a C.P.O. in the coast guard, but don't know what department.

Thanks again for the things you sent me.

Lovingly your daughter
Lynette

---

813 E. Call St.
Tallahassee, Fla
Jan 10, 1944

Dear Dad,

I have settled down to work again in school. Dora Ann gave me a Sterling silver belt buckle with B ingraved.

Boy it sure is cold down here.

I am still captain of the patrol Boys last week we got shirts, Belts the kind that go around your waist and then over your shoulder, ties, badges, caps, and coats. I sure enjoyed being with the six days you were home. I ... that this thing will soon be with and you can come home stay.

Sorry I didn't make two paragraphs out of what I about the patrols and you I did it before I thought.

We are getting between and 8 eggs a day now.

Blondie is just as as ever but don't stink so much.

Well I must close
Love,
Bud

Courtesy Bernhardt Leynes

I Was a Ten-year-old Mascot at Panama Canal

John E. Schmidt, Jr., Maryland

During the Depression, it was very difficult to work. My father and mother were both employed by Bell Telephone Company in our hometown of Baltimore, Maryland. It was there on the bulletin board that my father found a sign about employment in the Panama Canal with the U.S. Army Signal Corps. I do not know the details, but my father decided to give it a shot. He went down in 1934 to become a civilian employee, and the following year my mother and sister and I followed.

Since my father was working for the Army, we had no place to live at the time. We moved into what my mother called a converted paint shack. The floors were dirt and hard. Pieces of drapery material were put up to partition off each room. The interesting thing, what initiated me into the military atmosphere, was it was set right in the middle of a set of Army barracks at the Post of Corozel. There is a picture of me at 4 years old, and I am dressed in a khaki uniform with 2nd lieutenant bars that the soldiers had made for me.

With the more service each man put into the Army, the better quarters his family was assigned. Thus, we shortly moved to a new home in the town of Pedro Miguel in 1941. I was just 10 years old then and I vividly remember the influx of military forces of all varieties. It was obvious to us living there that Pedro Miguel was heavily defended with anti-aircraft and basically 40 millimeter barrel size. An incredibly dense arrangement of barrage balloons was practically on every corner of our town. When I walked to church, I could look to my left at the ball park and see a barrage balloon site.

At Cerro Luisa, the cut from the enormous hill behind Pedro Miguel, there was a torpedo bomber net hung by the military. It was incredible to look at because it simply appeared to be a large tennis court net. The only difference was that it was solid at top and hundreds of cables hung down from it. The concept was that if a torpedo bomber from Japan tried to get a torpedo into the locks, the only way they could possibly do it would be to come down low on that cut and lob it. The net was fixed in a place where a plane flying by would probably collide with it. Of course, we never were torpedoed, but an O47, an observation aircraft, crashed into it one day. It flew by and somehow tipped its wheels on the net and went up into the jungle. It eventually crashed. I remember going to the site and observing the wreckage. Two people were killed, but one survived.

The presence of war was all around us, but it was different for us children. We thought the barrage balloons were a wonderful thing, but the parents, being older and smarter, hated them. They did not like the smudge pots, but we enjoyed them completely. The concept was that if an attack did come, they would set off the smoke pots, preventing aircrafts from seeing. It was a significant defense in those days. To the innocent, the frequent tests provided games and entertainment. When one was set off, we would run through the massive smoke screens and hide from each other. The most exciting memory I have, historically speaking, was being able to sit at the edge of the locks, or even go into them, and watch the ships come through. Ships continuously flowed through the town and the bridge at Miraflores locks would frequently open, causing traffic to stop on the west bank of the canal. It often caused many students to be late for school because we were on the western bank and school was on the east. We just could not get there.

I would say that some of the big highlights of my growing up, the most significant was that I grew incredibly close with friends of the Army groups around Pedro Miguel. I became a mascot, truly a mascot. I did not wear a uniform, but I used to go to all the activities in the battery there. On payday, I would sit there with the 1st Sergeant and help him at pay call. It was exciting.

There were countless times that I would go with the jeep into the hills where they had batteries strung around there on feed runs. From the mess hall down at the main battery, they would fix the chow in metal containers and then we would carry it to the men up on of the hills. I was only a little guy, about 10 years old doing this.

In 1978, still on active duty, I was reading a Reserve Officer's magazine and saw an article about trying to locate people. I thought to myself, "Well, I'll try that." I sent a letter following up on it and shortly thereafter I received a phone call. The call came from a man who was the battery commander back in the days of WWII. He was a retired officer and had also seen the ad in the ROA magazine. We talked for an hour afterward about the days back in the Canal Zone of Pedro Miguel.

Saying Goodbye to a Loved One

Lucille Barrett, Connecticut

Closely Watched Trains

Something in me doesn't love a train.
Leaning on your uniform breast
crests of buttons press my cheek,
your breath hangs in my hair
Hefting the khaki sack
you will board.

I wait while the Santa Fe lurches
you're leaning against a pane
wheels hunch the tracks
moaning like madmen.
Troops of telephone poles flee
before the hooting of track
Your arm weightless as memory
smaller and smaller, waves
to the retreating platform.
It's a fast parting.

There is something in me
that doesn't trust trains,
the guttural commands of rails
the gasps of an engine
the over trail of ash.

***

Heartstrings pull to the breaking point as the troop train pulls from a station.

Saying goodbye to a loved one bound for war has been repeated thousands of times, and carries with it a lifetime of proud and sad memories. It matters not when, where, or what country, surely this experience is equal in intensity of emotion!

Lucille Barrett's poetry touches on this delicate occasion.

Mourning the Death of a Living Soldier

Terri Webster, Vermont

My father-in-law, Donald, was captured at the Battle of the Bulge during WWII and was a prisoner of war. He entered the service in March of 1943 and was stationed at North Camp Polk, Louisiana. He went overseas in May 1944, joining the glider infantry of the 101st airborne division and was awarded the Purple Heart in September for wounds received in Holland. Donald had been hospitalized and once recovered, sent back into action. After only a few days, though, he was reported missing. His parents were sent a telegram notifying them that their son was M.I.A. A few days, perhaps weeks, later they were sent another telegram confirming that he had died. Newspapers printed out articles of the P.F.C. Webster, telling the traumatic tale of his being killed in Belgium on December 26th. His mother was pregnant at the time and suffered a miscarriage due to the heart-breaking news.

Memorial services were held in his honor since there was no body to bury. Months later, on March 31st, a miracle came to Donald's parents when they received a letter from their son saying he was alive and doing well.

> I am in an American hospital in England now, and am sorry to have not been able to write to you for so long, but due to circumstances it has been impossible to write.
>
> If everything goes right, I should be home soon. I am getting very good care here.
>
> I hope this finds you well. I am having a Red Cross girl write this letter for me because I am too weak right now. Don't write to me until I send you my permanent address.
>
> Say "hello" to the folks around home for me. I will write again just as soon as possible.
>
> Love and kisses to all.

He had managed to escape from the POW camp. His parents were in a state of shock and even disbelief that this could be their son. It suddenly became real, however, when they received a telegram that stated:

> I am pleased to inform you that a corrected report has been received from the theater of operations which states that your son, private first class has been released from German Hospital and was not, repeat, not killed in action 26 December as you were previously informed. Letter follows.

Newspapers and radio announcements all told of this incredible story. One paper even described my father-in-law's story as one of the strangest during WWII. It made everyone question our government, wondering why it would write of Donald's death if he were still alive. His letters were analyzed for signs that it really was him, such as sayings, salutations, and inquiries about his sisters. Everything seemed to piece together, building up a renewed hope in both his parents.

Mrs. and Mrs. Webster were hesitant upon making these letters public because they feared it would bring a futile hope to all other parents who had been told their sons were killed in action. It was not a futile hope for them, however, when their Donald returned home to them, and shared his tale of surviving World War II.

Fifty years later, another miracle occurred. Donald located his wartime sweetheart Cynthia who lives in England. They had met in England before he was shipped to Belgium during the war. This rediscovery started letter writing which then led to nightly transatlantic phone calls resulting in a decision that she would fly to America for a reunion in 2004. Cynthia made the trip twice, but unfortunately, Donald has since passed away, ending this storybook romance.

Journal Notes from a College Student

Helen Toles Buffington, Georgia

So this is war. This hustle-bustle, hurrying world we live in today. Seems like everything is speeded up and, of course, it is. It has to be so we can win this war.

I am an American, an American who is experiencing war for the first time. This war is making us of the younger generation grow old fast, and who can help it? We've watched the happy-go-lucky America of peacetime plunge whole-heartedly into winning the war.

I remember distinctly December 7, 1941. It was a pretty, sunny, tropical day here in Georgia. Mother, daddy, and Hazel were out in the back yard enjoying the late afternoon. I decided to listen to the radio a few minutes and settled down in a comfortable chair near the radio. Gee, that was peaceful music, so beautiful and kind of suited my mood. Then an announcer interrupted the program to bring "a news bulletin." This wasn't unusual because something was always happening "over there." The announcer said, "Pearl Harbor has been bombed, many killed."

I didn't even know where that was and just decided it was somewhere in England. They were always having bombings. But my mind became very alert when he said, "Japan has announced that she considers herself in a state of war with (the) U.S."

I was stunned. Why, this was America; didn't they know who they were jumping on? As soon as I realized that it was true, I ran out the back door and told the folks. I guess I'll never forget that day. We came in and listened to the radio to get the details. There were many questions in our minds. Why did they jump on us? What could it profit them? They'd always been pretty good neighbors. What prompted such an outrageous act? Why, that skunk in Germany, of course! Hitler had "pushed" Japan on our back to take care of us while he carried out "his plans" in Europe.

The next day at school everyone was excited. "What would happen now?" we asked. I think most of us expected the Japs to march into New York any minute. That's how little we knew of war. Our professor arranged to get a radio for the students to hear the president declare war. We assembled in the large gymnasium and everyone was very quiet while the president delivered his message.

For the next few days, I don't expect we did very much studying. I really don't remember because I was as excited as any of the rest of the high school kids.

Many of the boys volunteered for service. More were being drafted and a lots (sic) of changes were taking place.

There wasn't much Christmas spirit that year, although everyone tried to appear gay and cheerful.

Seems like the Japs were getting the best of us in every battle. Many of our boys were leaving never to see the good old U.S. again. Since I have no brothers, I wasn't affected personally by this, although it did make me sad to think of any going through the torture they must. But in January, Harold Toles, my first cousin, joined the toughest branch of service, the Marines. I didn't think much about it at the time because so many were "joining up." And I didn't know anyone who had been killed or wounded in war.

***

In the last of February, Aunt Molly Weaver, my grandmother's step-mother, received a message from the War Department that her son (grandmother's half-brother) was missing in action. He was a sailor on the famous *Houston* and until this day we don't know whether he is captured or dead. Maybe after this war, he like many of our boys will come marching back after enduring the torture as a prisoner of war. I was at my grandmother's when Uncle Guy came over to tell her the bad news. She and (Aunt) Blanche were visiting neighbors when he came but he delivered the news to us, and was still there when they came home. They noticed something was wrong when granddad told them; (Aunt) Blanche slipped into the bedroom and I could see she was crying. However, grandmother was brave and sat there very quietly, but determined looking. There have been many days I'll never forget and that is one.

***

Later, J.C. Cavin, another cousin, was called as he had had training at a military college. J.C. went in as a Second Lieutenant and has recently been promoted to Captain.

In the last of April, Harold came home and stayed from the 25th to the 29th. I had the measles and did not get to see him but twice. The first time he came by with his folks on Sunday night. He was pretty cheerful but I knew it was unreal. He told us he expected to go soon after he got back.

Then they came by on the next Wednesday night as he'd started to catch a bus to leave. Everyone was on the verge of tears, I guess, except me. I just didn't understand how awful it was, I guess. I do now. When they went out to leave, Harold lingered behind the rest to tell me good-bye. I guess I realized then he was the nearest thing to a brother I'd ever have and I became really and truly sorry he had to go.

I got just one letter from him before he went overseas. It was a very blue letter, and I could tell he knew something big was going to happen even though he didn't know what.

The next news we had from him was a postcard stating his address. Through July and August he wrote but couldn't tell where he was. We guessed everywhere. We knew there were lots of Marines on Guadalcanal going through hell but I just couldn't believe he was there. Maybe it was because I didn't want to.

Then he wrote telling where he was. Guadalcanal! I was suddenly afraid, but I tried to assure myself he was alright (sic) because he wrote that he was having fun. Maybe he wasn't in the thick of fighting, I decided.

I got just one letter from him while he was on Guadalcanal. It was dated September 6th. Said he hadn't had time to fish any (that's his hobby), but he had seen plenty of big ones.

I always hate to even think of this. But a few weeks later a message from the War Department said he was wounded. I don't know how I studied during those weeks. Why, Harold was practically my brother. Oh, why did he even join anyway. If he hadn't joined he would be here today safe and well and not, not, no, no, I mustn't think that. We had good doctors to take care of our boys but I thought it anyway—He might be lying in those jungles dying—maybe they couldn't find him. Maybe there wasn't any medicine. Oh, maybe everything. I had to trust that he'd be all right. I was 14 then and I guess I didn't stop to figure things out, that they'd notify us if anything happened.

The last of November, Thanksgiving Day to be exact, Uncle Guy (Harold's father) received word from the Navy Department that Harold was admitted to the Naval Hospital in Mare Island, California, on November 13. This was really a day for giving thanks to the Almighty for sparing the life of this, one of the toughest leathernecks. In a few days, Harold himself wrote, saying he'd been hit by shrapnel in his right shoulder, and his arm wasn't much use to him. From then on we heard from him regularly.

Through his letters, we got a bird's eye view of what it was like on Guadalcanal. He thought he'd gotten at least twenty Japs, maybe twenty-five.

***

Then the Yanks marched into Africa in November and there were many comments on this big second front.

Recently, I saw a movie on the North African war theatre and I was especially impressed by the way our boys smiled into the camera. They were confidently sure of victory and in a civilized country. This picture, *At the Front*, was very different from another war picture, *We Are the Marines*, which I saw. The latter concerned the South Pacific theatre mostly and the boys, our gallant Marines, weren't so sure of victory. How could they be when America had lost every other major battle prior to that? Who but tough Yanks could stand to live for three weeks on two tablespoons of rice twice a day? We must admit it took courage, and a good leadership for them to take and hold that important base.

On the other hand, the African front had better advantages. Although many were killed and wounded, there were many less causalities than had been expected.

***

In January of '43, our president and the Prime Minister of England met in Casablanca. They said "unconditional surrender" and they had the best boys in the world to back them up.

***

Fletcher Toles, Harold's younger brother, was drafted into the Army on February 2, 1943 and put in the Coast Artillery.

A most wonderful thing happened in April, all of my three first cousins who were in the service were home at the same time.

Harold came first. A telegram came telling when he would leave. Another came saying he was delayed two days. We counted the days and didn't expect him to get here as early as he did.

Mother and daddy went to work as usual that Wednesday morning and at lunch they to (sic) school after Hazel and me saying Harold had come home the night before. Were we thrilled! It'd been so long since we'd seen him, just a year, but to him and us every day seemed like a year.

As we walked into the house, we saw a slender, tall, blond-headed boy sitting on the divan. I was astonished at the change that had come over Harold. He had a wild look in his eyes, it was seldom he smiled, he talked differently, and the greatest change was how aged he had become. But later I learned that he was very tired from his trip across the continent and after a rest he was better although he never lost completely that peculiar look.

After the situation was told to Fletcher's officers he was given a furlough. About the same time J.C. got a furlough, this made all the boys in the Toles family who are in the service home. Fletcher had grown taller than Harold and J.C. had gained many pounds.

The things Harold told brought tears to my eyes. How they landed just before dawn; how they slept in mud, with rain falling in their eyes and many more things that are so terrible it's best not to mention them.

***

We are rationed on sugar, coffee, gasoline, shoes, and canned food. None of this affects us very much but some people grumble anyway.

We have WACS, WAVES, SPARS, and Women Marines, and although there has been much criticism about our women in service, I think they are doing good work.

***

Last of July 1943, Mussolini was ousted. This is good news to us, because we know the Italians (not Fascists) don't really want to fight any more than we do, but were driven by the Germans and Fascists. In *At the Front*, an African war picture, the Italian prisoners smiled into the camera, but those Nazis, no sir, they were resentful.

One cannot turn on the radio and listen to *any* program without in some way or another being reminded that we are in war. Neither can we carry on a conversation with anyone without the subject of war being brought up. When we were first in the war, I had to remind myself every day that we *were* in war.

***

I write several service men and they have a cheerful outlook. Some people think a girl shouldn't write strange boys; however, I believe if she is writing to bring a little cheer into a soldier's, a sailor's or a Marine's life, it's the least any girl can do to keep the boys' morale up.

We're on our way to victory and although we aren't *too* optimistic now, we know in the end victory will be ours. There will be times when we won't make progress very fast, but there *will be* times when *are* (sic) making progress.

***

Many songs have been composed since the start of this war. I'll name a few I particularly like. "Praise the Lord and Pass the Ammunition;" "This is the Army, Mr. Jones;" "I've Got Gobs of Love!;" "You'll Never Know;" "Let's Remember Pearl Harbor;" "Any Bonds Today;" "You'd Be So Nice To Go Home To;" "I'm Getting Tired So Can I Go To Sleep;" "I Left My Heart at the Stage Door Canteen."

There's no reason for anyone to be hungry nowadays. There are plenty of jobs for everyone. Most of the school girls are working while school is out.

Before long all the senior boys of '42–'43 will be in service and when the girls become old enough, Lyerly High may have a daughter in the service.

***

Very often our Army planes zoom across the sky, and everyone runs out to watch "Uncle Sam's boys" fly over. We are proud of our "silver birds" as they fly across a deep blue sky, and we know that sooner or later those same planes will drop bombs over Tokyo (sic) or some other important target and help to bring justice to the world.

We read and hear about the people in Nazi-occupied countries suffering—the Poles, Czechs, Dutch, Belgians, and those brave French. I especially like the Dutch. They are so peace-loving and to have those Nazis come down and overrun a nation that wouldn't have harmed anyone, makes every true American want to fight this war to a finish.

***

The war is very good today September 28, 1943. The Russians are within 200 miles of old Polish border. The American 5th and British 8th are going slowly but surely on and today captured a large air base. We are progressing nicely in the South Pacific. Mussolini is reported to be in Rome but he won't be there long enough.

The father draft bill is trying to be delayed by ?? (sic) Wheeler, KY, at least till first of the year.

***

This September 7, 1943, last night Harold, Fletcher and Lamar came and ate supper with us. Oh, it was so nice to have them here. Together, those two boys who are almost as close a (sic) would be, to me, it was grand but not grand either, because they may never be together again. That's what war does, separates families, and makes men out of what are boys in peacetime.

It's now about 5:30 and Fletcher leaves about 7:00 P.M. They are coming by here going to the bus. I have a very different feeling than that which I had when Harold left. When Harold left we had been in war a few days over three months and we didn't have much of an idea of war; but now we are in the very middle of things. We know 500 men have been killed in Italy so far, and victory can't be ours for a long time not until we've done our utmost. First it was "Do your bit for the war effort," then "You've done your bit, now do (your) best." Now it is "You've done your best, do more."

Well, Fletcher *didn't* come by here and gee it's awful not seeing him again but maybe there's a reason.

***

Today, word came that Wake Island was being bombarded by Allies; no details were given.

We are slowly progressing on Italian front and we'll soon be in Rome. What'll be left when the Germans get through looting and they'll probably burn it. We'll make them pay, a thousand times, yes, if they aren't human enough to leave a little of the beautiful paintings and art which constitute greater Rome.

The Italians, bless their hearts, they are brave and real fighters. It was word over the radio that one Italian girl had thrown grenades from a roof onto Germans; she was one of many who sacrificed their lives for a good cause, democracy.

***

June 6, 1944—D-Day. Yes, at last the long-awaited invasion of the Nazi-controlled European western coast has begun. Today is one of the most important days of the world's history. The largest fleet and reinforcements ever to have been assembled was assembled last night to begin the Allied march to Berlin. Rome fell only last weekend and when the invasion followed it my prediction came true. On the radio NBC has had *very* few programs, only news flashes as they came in. Correspondents spoke from Washington, New York, and London. King

George spoke at 2:00 P.M. General Montgomery also spoke at about noon. Mr. Churchill made several comments. Our own wonderful President Roosevelt speaks at 9:00 tonight. People assembled for prayer at 11:00 A.M. in the Siville churches this morning. At intervals (on the radio) rabbis, priests, archbishops and preachers prayed and organ music was also heard. There seems to be less talk about it than expected but a certain subtle air hangs in the atmosphere. We are glad, yet we feel for those who gave their lives to make this attack possible. They are gallant, and we praise the Almighty for their courage and sacrifice. We appreciate them so much.

This is it—today, today, not yesterday, nor the day before, but *today*, June 6, 1944. This may be the day that will change the destiny of the world. We may be the nation to have the greatest part in this change. We want some things changed, yes certainly some people's way of thinking needs to be changed but we can hardly do that so we are out to stop their thinking.

***

June 15—1:30 a bulletin came in saying B-29s had bombed the Japanese homeland. This thrills me. Daddy is helping make those B-29s. They are being built in Georgia; now they help destroy Japan!

MY DIARY

August 11, 1945
We feel that soon, very soon perhaps the end of World War II is to come. Before last week, we felt sure the war would continue at least through 1945. Not so much now! That was *before* we, the general public, knew about the atomic bomb. Early last week, our plans flew over Hiroshima, in Japan, and unloaded one of these great bombs. The city was practically wiped off the map with just *one* bomb. Surely, we thought, Japan can "see the light"; surely she can see what we can and *will* do if she insists on being stubborn. Why, with a few hundred of these bombs we could literally destroy the Japanese race. We have plenty of these bombs, too. There are several factories that produce this bomb, one being located in the mountains of Tennessee, at Oak Ridge. The production of this bomb has been highly guarded. President Truman did not know if its existence until he took the office of president.

On August 9 came the wonderful news that Russia had declared war on Japan. That *really* was good news. At about the same time, came the announcement that another atomic bomb had been dropped in Japan, destroying many war factories there.

When President Truman, Prime Minister Atlee, and Generalissimo Stalin met at Potsdam, Germany recently, Russia agreed to enter the war by August 16. However, for reasons unknown here, she sped up the day of entry. When someone called into the office telling us this good news everyone became very happy. Some of the girls had tears flowing down their faces, tears of joy. How wonderfully happy we are that the course of events during the last three years has led us to shed more tears of joy and less tears of sorrow.

The entire world became alive yesterday when Japan announced that she was ready for surrender *if* the Emperor could remain. Many people thought yesterday would be our last day building B-29s (I was working at Bell Bomber plant at the time). People were in a gay, excited, and expectant mood. They could hardly control their gay spirits. The day wore on with still no important developments.

At noon today, it was announced over the radio that we were broadcasting our answer to Japan. What is our answer? Let's hope it is "Nothing but unconditional surrender." We've fought for three long, hard, bitter years. Now when it is almost over, why should we compromise? It'll take only a little more to make them give up unconditionally. God help that we make them do it!

When peace does come, let us not forget Pearl Harbor; let us not forget that only one ship, the *Arizona*, escaped unharmed; let us not forget that "death march"; and also, let us not forget we are a civilized Christian race. Yes, we will remember that fateful day in December 1941, when the Japs mercilessly attacked us, a neutral country. Never can we forget Wake Island, Manila, Bataan, and many other places that were overrun by Japan. Then our troops landed in Africa; they fought there; and they won there. There was Sicily, Salerno, and Rome; then D-Day. D-Day, yes, D-Day; the day that climaxed the European war. That was just a little over a year ago. Much, very much, has happened in this last year. We landed on the Normandy beaches; we fought across France; but in December came the Battle of the Bulge. Things looked dark then; darker than they had looked for a long time. Finally, we did *win* that battle and stormed across Germany. The Red Army was pushing across Poland and Germany from the other side. Then the Americans and Russians (sic) armies linked. More fighting; then we were in Berlin.

The entire world was stunned and shocked on April 12, 1945 at the news of the sudden death of Franklin Roosevelt. How *could* we go on without him? He was the life, the living symbol of democracy and our great country. We have missed [him] sorely; but his spirit can never be missed; his spirit lives and shall continue to live to guide us and keep us in the way of democracy.

***

On May 8, 1945 came the long-awaited V-E Day. It was the most wonderful news to come out of this war; but we Americans could not whole-heartedly rejoice at this victory. We had sons, brothers, husbands and fathers dying in the Pacific front. How much longer would this war with Japan go on? Some high officials predicted that it would probably last until the latter part of 1946. Another year of war? We were tired, very tired of war, but we must fight on! We must lick those Japs and then, only then could we really celebrate a victory.

Well, maybe it won't be so long until we can truly celebrate the victory. In the good old American way, we shall celebrate; but after the big hurrah, we won't settle immediately back to the pre-war type of peace. Our boys won't come back within a few weeks after V-J Day. It'll be months, maybe longer before some will return. Some will never return. Some are in the miry jungle swamps; some rest in the bottom of the ocean; others are under Japanese soil. These will never return. They gave their all that we can continue to live in freedom. They've won the war and we must win the peace.

Tomorrow morning we are going to have real biscuits for breakfast. We've been eating buns from the store because of the scarcity of lard. Yesterday Hazel got two pounds; so for a Sunday treat, we'll have genuine biscuits. Food of many kinds was quite scarce. Meat has been almost as rare as diamonds. Once last week we had pork chops. Mother has fried her boiling meat a few times to eat. It seems that meat is slowly becoming more plentiful. Many times we have searched every grocery and market in town for meat but no success. Real black pepper, mayonnaise, custard powders, soap powder, cigarettes, good candy, sugar (we used saccharin tablets), and some canned foods are rarities now too.

August 14, 1945
Victory! V-J Day at 6 CWT (Central War Time) this PM, President Truman announced the formal surrender of Japan! We went to town and celebrated. Celebrations will continue for two days. Oh gee, how wonderful! After three years and more than eight months of war with Japan, we are again at peace tonight.

From German Immigrant in 1927 to Doctorate in 1956

Norman Jasper, Florida

I came to the United States from Germany in 1932 when I was just 9 years old. My artist father had come a few years earlier in 1927. My family's departure from Germany had nothing to do with the Nazis; they were not in power at that point. They came to power just after . . . I was lucky. I left in the summer of 1932, and the Nazis took over in the fall. There was an election. And I think Hitler became Chancellor in January the next year.

I went to a public school in Brooklyn and high school. I went to the school of business—The Baruch School of Business—for a year. I was bored to death. Then I took up engineering at the City College of New York. I graduated as a mechanical engineer in June 1941, but I already had a job before I graduated. I got an appointment as a Naval architect at the Puget Sound Naval Shipyard in Bremerton in the state of Washington. I spent the war years from 1941 to 1946 in that shipyard in the scientific and test group. I started as a junior naval architect, and in the years I was there, I worked for that particular group.

I remember Pearl Harbor very well. I was a naval architect at Puget Sound, and we were out camping. On our way home from camp, there was an announcement on the radio that the Japanese had bombed Pearl Harbor. On the west coast, we had to keep the lights down and all the windows were blacked out. We worked six days a week after that, maybe even before that.

I studied all the time while I was employed, in various colleges and universities. I got my master's degree at the University of Maryland in engineering and mathematics. I received my doctorate degree in aeronautical engineering at Catholic University. I took post-doctorate courses and was a Fellow at the Sloan Institute for Advanced Engineering Studies for a sabbatical year.

When I first got to Puget Sound, we were building so-called AVPs. They were aircraft rescue vessels. I was involved in studying the stability of them and finally launching these AVPs. After I became a member of the scientific and test group. In this group, I was involved in resolving some of the most complex problems. One of the earliest problems that remain a puzzle to me concerned our battleships. The navy had old battleships like the *Alabama*, which had "cage masts" made out of piping, while the newer battleships, like the *North Carolina*, had build-up superstructure "masts." Our study was a very complex investigation of the stress distribution in this cage mast. The cage mast would have the range finders and radars on top. For some reason, we had to study the stress distribution on them, but didn't know what the consequences of our work would be. We performed a very complex stress analysis and testing on these masts. After all the testing was done, it had to be analyzed and reported. They then proceeded to cut the cage mast off and replace it with the superstructure mast that was on newer battleships.

Another area that I worked on was very interesting. All of our ships were built in peace time, and they were not designed to handle the shock from underwater explosions. Once we got into war, our ships were under torpedo attacks as well as mining attacks. The shock from these explosions or even the shock from heavy impact of the ships' on waves would cause the supports of equipment to crack. It was my job to check the ships to determine whether they were properly shock mounted. If the equipment wasn't, I determined what was required, and made the recommendations for proper installation.

The civilian force at Puget Sound was around 30,000. The technical staff was relatively small. The shipyard was a large facility, and our group consisted of about fifteen members. The entire technical staff probably had about 150 or so naval architects, engineers, and so forth.

When I came out west, the war hadn't started yet, but they were already getting ready. I had been married my last year in college, but my wife wasn't with me. I couldn't find an apartment or a room, so I stayed at the YMCA for a couple of days. Then I got a room at a hotel and my wife joined me later. We rented one of these efficiency apartments where the bed was in the wall. We had about eighteen different places we stayed in about five years. We even bought a trailer to stay in. Finally, the Navy or the government built housing for people working in the shipyard. We finally got into one of those, and our life improved. Our situation was pretty nice once we had a home and neighbors, but before that, it was pretty rough. There were enforced blackouts, and you had these barrage balloons up. Everything was blacked out at night.

I feel that I could have been more useful at the Pearl Harbor shipyard. I tried to go when they had the attack at Pearl Harbor, but I had punctured eardrums, so I was classified as 4-F. When Pearl Harbor occurred, they wanted people from the United States, naval architects, and so on to come over. They needed more staff, so I volunteered. Unfortunately, they wouldn't take me on account of my punctured eardrums. I tried but they said "You might need a doctor's attention." So I didn't get to go.

Waiting for MIA News

Gordon P. Brown, Texas

One of the hardest aspects of the home front was the agonizing wait for news about the MIAs. TS Gordon Brown was reported missing in action. About two weeks later his family heard from him that he was in a hospital in Italy. These two letters (one written on November 2, 1944 and the other November 5, 1944) were written shortly after receiving the good news. They are from his mother expressing her joy and relief.

Sunday Nov. 5, 1944

Hello Son!

How are you today? I sure wish
I had the answere to that question right now
all thou I am not worry like I was last
week, and the week before, I still wonder
how you are and where you are. I guess I'll know
all about it some day, but, now I want to know
about you.

Do you know what excitement you caused in
these two town. Patty was here when her mother
called and told us the news, that you were
missing in action, how the news got over
the towns so quick I dont know but before
night the phone began to ring and it hasint
stoped yet, the first two weeks people called to
say how sorry they were to hear the bad news
and since they called to say how glad they
are that you got back, and they want to
know all kinds of things which I cant tell
them because I dont know myself. I recieve
any number of cards and letters expressing their
sympathy, the pastor Rev. Wones called the first
Sunday afternoon and brought a large
armfull of yellow chrysanthemus that had
been on the altar during church service

Courtesy Gordon P. Brown

and I understand they prayed for you during the service, and in the afternoon here at the house the Roes, Doris, Patty and I bowed our head while Rev. Wones had prayer he called again on Tuesday of this last week, you know Gordon I never knew that you and your Dad and I had so many friends both in the church and the 2 towns, but the last few weeks shows we have. This morning Rev. Wones prayed for the recovery of Gordon Brown who had been missing and was now in the hospital. You know Gordon all my life I have been a believer of prayer but never have I been so glad of it as I have been these last few weeks for that was all I had the days you were gone I'm glad I was'nt like the man who when in trouble said, Dear God I never bother you before and if you help me now I'll never bother you again, of course that meant to be funny but it would'nt have been funny for me if I could not have asked God to help you and me to, as I have done each day since you came to stay with me allmost twentyfive years ago and an extra special prayer each day for you and the men on your plane.

Write as often as you can and tell me all about yourself. The Love and Prayers of one who Loves you go with you allways Mom

Courtesy Gordon P. Brown

Nov. 2, 1944

Hello Son

       your letter came today, I cant tell you how glad I am you got back, you know I never could put my emotions into words, let alone put them down on paper, but you do know how much I love you, and what you mean to me, you are my world, everything, so you can guess how I felt when word came you were missing, the light of my world went out, for two weeks I knew you were'nt coming back but I never stoped praying that God would hold on to your right hand and bring you and the boys safely back (remember that one line of pray I used to write you when you were in Alaska, I, Jehovah thy God, will hold thy right hand, saying unto thee, Fear not; I will help thee.) that was my pray, but, not for me but for you and the boys.

But today is Christmas, for me the lights are on all over my world, I'm like a feather flowting on the breeze, I'm so happy I cant hardly sit still long enough to write, I want to shout it from the house tops, my son is back, my son is safe, but I wont I dont want the neighbors to think I've lost my mind with joy, but, I am going to phone ever one I know just as soon as I sign my name to this letter, I write again tomorrow

Courtesy Gordon P. Brown

Take good care of yourself and write soon to one who loves you always

Your
Mom

Courtesy Gordon P. Brown

Part 2

It Was a Time for ... Caution and Prejudice

Nerves were on edge. We were told, "Expect the unexpected!" Would America's west coast be invaded by Japan, and what advances would Germany make on the east coast? Many American citizens of Japanese and German descent were interned in camps as a "safeguard" against sabotage. Conscientious objectors to the war (and draft) were sent to serve in remote areas of forestry preserves far from the battlefield. African Americans were segregated in the military service of their country. Many women serving the cause as factory workers were at first greeted with skepticism and some disrespect by male counterparts for the intrusion into their pre-war territory.

Anger and frustration were easily aroused, so issues of a controversial nature were kept low key to retain high morale. The only thing "normal" was the constant reminder that we were at war and that we had to stretch food and gasoline coupons. Emotions were in high gear as thoughts of far-away battlefields dominated our lives.

The people who lived through World War II are often referred to as the "Greatest Generation," but we were certainly not the "perfect" generation.

Subway passenger reads news about Pearl Harbor attack. [Courtesy Westport Public Library]

THE WHITE HOUSE
WASHINGTON

A monetary sum and words alone cannot restore lost years or erase painful memories; neither can they fully convey our Nation's resolve to rectify injustice and to uphold the rights of individuals. We can never fully right the wrongs of the past. But we can take a clear stand for justice and recognize that serious injustices were done to Japanese Americans during World War II.

In enacting a law calling for restitution and offering a sincere apology, your fellow Americns have, in a very real sense, renewed their traditional commitment to the ideals of freedom, equality, and justice. You and your family have our best wishes for the future.

Sincerely,

GEORGE BUSH
PRESIDENT OF THE UNITED STATES

O C T O B E R   1 9 9 0

After 45 years, the United States government officially recognized the injustices experienced by the Japanese internees.

A Japanese American Interned

Gene Takahashi, Connecticut

Being a second generation Japanese American, i.e., a Nisei, has been a prominent aspect of my life both as a civilian and in the military.

I was born in a small farming community, Imperial Valley, in Southern California near the Mexican border. My family moved annually, which was the norm for vegetable and melon farmers. (Added to this fact is that Japanese were not allowed to own property.) I attended many schools, some of which were one-room schoolhouses.

Shortly before World War II, my father suffered a stroke and died while farming in the unbearable heat of the region. My mother and my siblings then ran a small lunch and grocery store across the street from El Centro High School. Life was simple and relatively free of complexity and discrimination.

All of this came to an abrupt end with the attack on Pearl Harbor and the declaration of war by the United States. The western halves of the states of Washington and Oregon, the entire state of California, and a small section of Arizona were placed under military rule, and subsequently, some 120,000 Japanese, 77,000 of whom were American citizens, were forced to leave the military zone under very short notice. They were herded into ten relocation or concentration camps which were hastily built. These camps, surrounded by barbed wire and patrolled by armed sentries, were usually located in desert or swamp areas, far from civilization and with few amenities. Most evacuees were imprisoned for three to four years. For my family, it was the harshest period of our lives.

After three years in camp, we were permitted to leave as long as we didn't go to the West Coast. My family chose to go to Cleveland, Ohio, since it was on a lake and obviously not desert land.

So, we started a new life with a great deal of trepidation in a new and strange environment with no prospects of jobs or a place to live.

We were able to find a small apartment in the Flats, the steel mill area. My stepfather had to take a very low-skill job. My sisters were afraid to go outside of the apartment. I attended a local high school where most of the students were Polish and the few graduates usually worked in the steel mills. Inexplicably, I was accepted and elected Class Treasurer. Ironically, the $2,000 I had to collect for the prom and graduation pictures was far more than our family had. I was able to get part-time jobs at sheet metal and steel barrel companies and helped contribute toward family expenses. Discrimination was definitely there but not structured because most Clevelanders weren't familiar with any Japanese and couldn't identify them. It took several years after the end of World War II for this underlying tension and hostility to dissipate.

As for the military, many of the Nisei who were over 18 years of age requested that a special segregated unit be activated so they could volunteer from the camps. These young Nisei were eager to show their loyalty to the United States. The 442nd Regimental Combat Team was organized in response and this group fought with great distinction in the European Theater becoming the most highly decorated unit in the Army. Other Nisei were recruited for Military Intelligence to act as interpreters in the Pacific, and this group, too, served with distinction.

I was too young to volunteer for the 442nd, but I, too, was highly motivated to prove my loyalty. So immediately after graduation from high school I signed up at the local Army recruiting station. However, after taking basic and special training and attending Officers Candidate School at Fort Benning, GA, the war was over and I could only serve as a platoon leader in the occupation of Korea. After my tour of duty I signed up for Army inactive reserves and returned to Cleveland where I earned my bachelor's degree in two and one-half years.

By this time the Korean War had begun and much to my surprise, upon graduating from college, I received a telegram from President Truman ordering my recall to active duty. Due to the strange fortunes of war I was rushed to combat duty with the Second Division. My wish to serve in combat was amply satisfied with 6 months at the front fighting the North Korean and Chinese armies. During this time, I received the Bronze Medal for valor, was taken prisoner by the Chinese and escaped, and was finally wounded and hospitalized for fourteen months. I felt that my dues had been paid.

Returning again to civilian life, I went back to school to earn a graduate degree. But once again, I faced discrimination as a minority person. So, in spite of a master's degree I had to resort to selling Fuller Brushes door to door to support my wife and family. Eventually, through scoring well on Civil Service Exams, I was able to get a job with the Navy Finance Center where I studied computer sciences, which was in its infancy. I was recruited by IBM where I served for some thirty-two years eventually becoming Director of Corporate Litigation. After retiring, I formed my own consulting group and continued in the litigation area for an additional ten years.

Having had the opportunity to have careers in both business and the military I find that they are fundamentally the same especially for a person in the so-called minority groups. One's status and eventual success requires extra drive and dedication toward stated goals. Of course, one is more dangerous than the other but I would be hard-pressed to say which is more difficult to achieve and cope with. In the end, it's the personal attributes which a person brings to a situation which determines his ability to adapt to the complexities and challenges which must be faced in a sometimes prejudicial and unforgiving atmosphere.

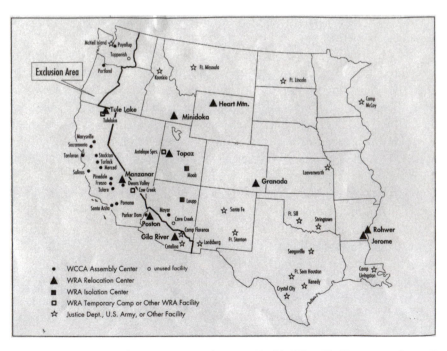

Japanese-American relocation sites during World War II [Courtesy Gene J. Takahashi]

Leaving home and friends, Los Angeles, CA, April 1942. [National Archives and Records Administration]

An American's Viewpoint of Internment Camps

Mary E. Williams, Arizona

The wartime hysteria that resulted from Pearl Harbor caused our government to fear there might be spies among us—that the west coast might be invaded. Consequently, the Federal Government established ten internment camps extending as far east as Arkansas, two of which held 20,000 Japanese Americans. These poor people were forced to leave their homes, farms, or businesses and all their possessions.

Boredom ran rampant through the adult camps and education programs were created for them. With help, they acquired many artistic as well as farming skills. Vegetable gardens soon evolved into a community effort. The internees cleared out nearly 600 acres of land outside the camp for cultivation. Others developed a drainage and irrigation system to draw water from the bayous. Due to their great success, surplus vegetables were sent to help other military installations and even the Veterans Administration Hospital.

During World War II a shortage of season farm workers developed in the states of Montana, Utah, Wyoming, and Idaho. The War Relocation Authority finally sent out a call to the camps for help. Dispersing around the country, the former internees accepted the task of helping out the country that had once imprisoned them. There was anti-Japanese sentiment in the designated work places and it was not easy for these Japanese Americans. However, it was an opportunity to get away from the dull routine of the camps.

The camp schooling was a success. Some of the instructors were of Japanese ancestry, and others were Caucasians hired to teach in the camps. Teachers recall that the students took an interest in their work, determined to see each assignment through until completion.

Cartoonists from the Walt Disney Studios came to teach the internees drawing. One student in particular was inspired, Ruth Asawa. She created a memorial sculpture to the Japanese Americans that were sent to the camps in World War II. The memorial was commissioned by the city of San Jose, California, and was dedicated in 1994.

By 1943, President Roosevelt issued a statement allowing young men of Japanese descent to enlist in a special army unit, and the 442nd Combat Team was formed at Camp Shelby, Mississippi. My husband, Maurice E. Williams, was one of the new 2nd Lieutenants sent there. The training was rugged, and the officers and men went through a great deal of combat together.

One of the first letters I received from my husband when he was overseas mentioned seeing one of the Seven Wonders of the World. I did know he was in Italy so I guessed he meant the Leaning Tower of Pisa. After the war, he informed me that they had used it for an Observation Post to call for fire on the Germans.

In October of 1944 the 442nd rescued a Lost Battalion of the 36th Texas Division. They rescued 211 men and suffered over 800 casualties. The 442nd liberated the town of Bruyeres in the Vosges Mountains of Southern France and to this day the folks are still grateful.

During the last year of World War II some of the Japanese Americans were allowed to move to areas of the Midwest to work; a suggestion named Cincinnati as a desired place of relocation. While some remained where they were, others returned to the west coast immediately after the war. They met with great difficulty despite their true loyalty to America. They were unwelcome, being spat at and called filthy names.

Children of the internees questioned their parents upon their arrivals back at home. "Why did you go?" they would ask. Our Nisei friends in Seattle told us that it was the children (or third generation) who instigated much of the redress to come which eventually led to the apology and reparation payments in 1988. The United States government saw the wrong they had done and publicly apologized to the internees, offering $20,000 in tax-free redress payments to each survivor. The Japanese Americans had also been offered 30 cents on the dollar for what had been taken away from them, though no price could ever be placed on what they had truly lost.

What's More Important, Pants or Your Soul?

Mozzelle Bearden Ivey, Georgia

I was listening to my neighbor's radio when it was broadcasted that Pearl Harbor had just been bombed. It sent shockwaves over everybody. I was 16 years old at the time and still going to high school in Ideal, Georgia. In 1942 I graduated with the common knowledge that the Warner Robbins Base was desperately looking for people to staff the depot that was being constructed.

I wanted to get away from home, a farm, and be on my own for once. And the money! Before the Second World War, the economy was in a deplorable state and I started working for $1,200 a year. My salary was impressive to me, at least, because I had never worked before. During the first year of work, I commuted sixty miles each day. It was an hour drive, carpooling with fellow employees. Every morning we left very early, often before the sun came up, and I would sleep in the car. It was exciting and new and I enjoyed each paycheck because it was my own. Having few expenses, living was easy for me.

The hiring procedure for Warner Robbins Base sent me to Macon where I took the Civil Service exam. I did well in every category but my eyesight. It was the first time that I learned my vision was poor, and of course, I had to get glasses before I could proceed. Twelve weeks of intensive engine repair training followed. The session covered general knowledge of how a gasoline-powered engine works. I never knew I could be interested in mechanical work, but I thoroughly enjoyed it.

After the twelve weeks, I was assigned to an engine repair unit. My only job was to take the 40-pound cylinders out of these giant planes and then grind the valve seats where the intake and exhaust valves came into the cylinders. Work was monotonous, but there was always someone to talk to. The noise was never too loud that the employees could not laugh and talk amongst the others around us. It was always pleasant.

The regular shifts at the base ran five days a week, from eight until four. I often worked the afternoon shift and found it to be much more preferable. During the time I worked the latter shift, my aunt and I were sharing an apartment with two other girls. We realized, though, that sleeping with someone else in the room during the daytime was virtually impossible. Thus, we packed up and moved to another apartment in Macon where we could be ourselves and not have to worry about other people roaming around the apartment.

The worst part about my job was being forced to stand the entire time. Kindly, though, the cylinders were raised to a level at which we did not have to strain our backs, bending down to lift them. Besides, I was 17, young and strong, and it did not bother me. The work was greasy, though! My hands were often covered and my hair streaked with it. It was required that I wore pants to work, but it seemed fitting, mandatory or not. When we ground the valve seats of the cylinder, a lubricant was spread over the machine to keep it from sparking. You could not help but wear it half the time. Our job was made easier, though, by our supervisory group. All males, they were not only incredibly kind, but cooperate and encouraging. No one ever pressured us into doing more than we could and everyone felt comfortable about her job.

One incident to demonstrate how narrow-minded people could be, involved a preacher and his wife. They operated a boarding house in which my brother, his wife, and young daughter lived. The preacher objected strenuously to my wearing pants when I entered the house. He demanded that I carry other clothes with me. I informed him that my job required wearing pants, but the preacher would not budge from his position. When I, too, refused to give in, he asked me, "What is more important to you, your soul or your job?" He was so close-minded that he condemned women wearing pants as a sin and here I was trying to help our country, which was at war. Of course, I told him that at that point, my job was the most important thing.

Conscientious Objector to the War

Gregg Phifer, Florida

Everyone played a role in WWII. Mine was as a Conscientious Objector. In June of 1941, I was in Iowa earning my master's degree. From then until 1942 I practiced as a teaching assistant. Afterward, I registered for the Selective Service in Iowa.

My father had registered as a CO during WWI. I grew up in Cincinnati's Westwood Methodist Church during a time when they strongly emphasized peace, maybe even pacifist. Most young men got over this feeling. I did not. My local board in Cincinnati refused to give me CO status, so I appeared before a hearing officer in Nashville, Tennessee. They asked questions, I gave answers, and finally, I was given what I asked for.

As a CO, one was assigned to Civilian Public Service, the CPS. The government was so disturbed by the COs of the First World War that they sent to prison many people who should not have been there: Mennonites, Brethrens, Quakers, and others. Our country was now involved in the world's second great war and they were determined this problem with the COs would not happen again. When it came to designing Selective Service during WWII, the feds consciously and deliberately made an effort to accommodate those Mennonites, Brethens, Quakers, and people like me who simply refused to participate in military service.

The public treated the COs well. We never really felt resentment or any particular criticism by our friends. Actually, Selective Service was anxious to get us off, away from everybody. We went to work for the Soil Conservation Service, the Forest Service, The Park Service— really most jobs that kept us away from people most of the time. Most COs had strong support back at home, myself included.

The government assigned each of us to a particular place. In my case, I was assigned to CPS 19, Buck Creek Camp in Marion, North

Carolina. It was administered by the American Friends Service Committee. In the beginning, all of the camps were overseen by one of the historic peace churches, in my case, the Friends.

I worked as a smoke jumper and in a way, that profession separated us from the criticized groups. Smoke jumpers had special relations because people recognized us as doing important and dangerous work. I think we had an easier time than many other COs. Newspaper stories in Spokane, Washington, actually praised those smoke jumpers identified as COs. Our work was fairly risky to both our lives and limbs. It was a hazardous occupation, but we were lucky in a way. We only had one unfortunate death. This was probably due to the fact that most of our jumper fires were relatively small, one or two dozen acres. I happened to jump on three very large fires. We could get to them faster than any truck could drive and we could stop it before it grew very big. Most of the five-state territory we worked had no roads. We would go in by plane and get to the point within an hour. A walk-in crew might have taken days to reach the fire. Our assignments were usually to pinch off a particular area, but sometimes we had to get out of the way before the fire flanked us.

I suppose one of the main reasons I was assigned to this position in the Forest Service was because I fought fires before I went to the smoke jumpers. At the second camp I went to, 37, in Coleville, California, the Forest Service was anxious to get a squad together which they could send anywhere in the region to fight fires. This was to be a highly trained group. I volunteered, but later on we were all let go because they had hired Mexican farm workers to do the job instead. I transferred to the Inyo National Forest in Northern California. You can see the pattern of our relocations—places we were not very visible to the public.

One time, I was putting some new soles on my boots. They had a tendency to wear out after a short while. I was scheduled to jump into Glacier National Park. I could have jumped there, but my shoes were not ready! They dropped me down to a lower list and I made the next jump somewhere in Idaho.

COs had two bosses. One was Selective Service, a government agency. The parallel agency from the churches was NSBRO—the National Service Board for Religious Objectors. Projects were jointly negotiated between the two, but there is no doubt that the Selective Service had the final say. An example of one agreement was the willingness of the Selective Service to allow a lot of COs to go into the mental hospitals, which was one of their main areas of service. If I had not gone to the smoke jumpers, I very possibly would have gone there. I saw that COs made quite a transformation in some mental hospitals.

There were a number of men in the CPS who were eccentric. For example, many were Jehovah's Witnesses. They considered themselves to be ministers and adamantly refused CPS assignment. As a result, many went to prison. However, a few of them wound up in CPS and I knew some of my friends at the Buck Creek Camp to be Jehovah's Witnesses. Since they considered themselves to be ministers, they were exempt from the draft and therefore did not remain in the CPS long.

I found it interesting that some assignees at Buck Creek were positively convinced that cooking in aluminum cookware was deadly. No one dared to use it because of them. The men even had demonstrations against this. They read us speeches at our evening supper about the dangers of the cookware. "No more aluminum cookware! It's gonna poison us all!"

CPS was basically intended to be for Religious Objectors, but there were a number who simply did not have that sort of religious background. Most did, but I found those released from prison had no care for it. I guess the reason for them being sent there was because the government did not want them in prison. It was the simplest and quickest thing to do. It interested me that some men were not willing to accept this offer. They would insist on remaining in prison instead, which they did. The rest of us that were out in the freedom of our country continued our work. Every day we prayed that it would, in fact, remain a free country.

Facing the War at Home as a 4-F

W.V. (Mac) McConnell, Florida

I had an inclination to become a forester so I enrolled in the School of Forestry in Pennsylvania State College—now Pennsylvania State University. I remember exactly where I was on December 7, 1941. I was a junior in college who had a hard Saturday night. That Sunday morning I rolled over in bed, recovering. At first there was very little change in what was happening at the college, but later on, the Army, and other services, used the facilities for training officer candidates. They took over fraternity houses and moved in trainees. Every morning I was awakened by the sound of them marching by and singing. We had the Selective Service and everyone at school registered for the draft. Those students with good grades were given student deferments. Presumably, there would be life after the war and the educated people, those with training, would be needed.

I was born in the smoky city, Pittsburgh, Pennsylvania, in a little suburb called Emsworth. My birth date was February 14, 1922. When I was 6 months old, my father passed away and I, along with four other children, was raised by my widowed mother. My mother had a difficult time because it was the Depression and some of the banks had closed down. My father was a civil engineer who died at an early age, 46. He was not in a very strong financial position, but my mother survived with our help. We each took on house chores and outside jobs.

There was very little conflict, in fact, very little contact between the officer candidate trainees and the so-called regular students. Pennsylvania State College was a land grant, so for the first two years everyone took ROTC. Those students had opted for a career in the Army or armed forces took an extra two years on top of the first. I was not one of those students, but most of my friends were.

Prior to December 7th, all college students thought that whatever was going to happen would happen to someone else. We knew in general that the world was in turmoil and Hitler was invading all these countries, but the situation was deteriorating. On the eighth of December, there was real recognition of this world affair in our day-to-day living. There was no particular concern, no anticipation, and no realization that soon the United States would be involved in this. I presume, judging from what happened at Pearl Harbor, that the leaders of our country did not have that foresight either.

After Pearl Harbor, everyone I knew went down and registered for the draft. I did end up registering, but was given a student deferment. After graduation I was classified as "Let's Go." I received the famous "greetings" letters and reported for induction. I was in Pittsburgh at the time, having graduated. There were several of us who took the train to Federal Street Station. At the induction center, we were stripped and examined. My eyesight was atrocious, even back then, and after the eye exam, I was considered a 4-F, which meant that I was medically unfit to serve. Most of the men I was with had been accepted and I was devastated. I had wanted to go.

Being young and patriotic, and perhaps a bit foolish, I thought this was going to be the chance of a lifetime and that if I had gone, nothing would happen to me. I remember thinking this was going to be the "great adventure" and if I missed out, I would have missed one of the most important events of my life, of my generation. Maybe I really did not think about everything at all. Being a 4-F was not a pleasant experience and eventually it did change. I was given a 1-AL which is limited service. This came a while later, though, due to the metamorphosis of the classification process over the years. Also, the selective service changed in order to accommodate different needs and different situations. I remained a 1-AL through the end of the war.

I applied for work in the Forest Service. It had lost most personnel to the armed services, so I was accepted. My first assignment was Mena, Arkansas, on the Ouachita National Forest. In getting my first assignment, my classification was SP-6 or 7, which is low. My annual salary was $2,400, which was not much even in those days, but you were not in this field for the money. I worked hard and soon became a junior forester.

At the time of the war, forestry work was much different than it is today. We were not concerned with aesthetics or red-cockaded woodpeckers. Our interest was getting the timber, putting out fires, and doing the job we had set out to do when joining the Forestry Service. Focus was placed on producing timber because the armed forces, and the nation, needed it. Timber was in demand to build pallets to ship items and barracks for the solders. Each district had to get thousands of board feet and we were dedicated to meeting our quota.

After a few months, I was transferred into the supervisor's office where I was a timber management staff assistant. Once again, my focus was on producing timber. There, I worked with the local ranger, going out and scaling logs.

In facing the war at home, there was still little immediate concern. We followed what was happening in the various theaters of war as things progressed, but it was not all-consuming, it was not *all* the time, unless you had relatives. I did. I had cousins who were involved, and sadly, one was killed. To others, unlike myself, the war was just some-thing of background noise that you knew was there. Everyone knew what they were doing was important and overall, I think it helped to create a sense of community, of common goals, and sharing values.

When the war ended there were still rationings and many adjust-ments to get used to afterward. However, there were no major shortages when we did ration later, and looking back today it does seem as if we lived without so much back then, but there was no feeling of depriva-tion or sacrificing. It was just a part of what needed to be done to help our country back on its feet once again.

The Riot that Brought an Army Together

Clarence Inniss, Louisiana

(Inniss was interviewed in August of 2000 by Joan Denman of the Institute on World War II and The Human Experience, Florida State University, Tallahassee, Florida.)

Denman: I thought if we could just sort of start a real basic thing. I'm sure you remember Pearl Harbor. What do you remember about your reactions and everybody's reactions around you? I mean, were you sort of expecting a war to break out or to be declared? Were you surprised about the Japanese attacking?

Inniss: Most surprised, because I hadn't been following too carefully prior to that. At the time, I was working at a service station approximately five miles from Jackson Barracks, and I was member of scrub football team that had scheduled a game against the soldiers at Jackson Barracks that particular Sunday. So that when I got off from work, I jumped on my bicycle and headed for Jackson Barracks. We had gone about one quarter into the game when there was a call for the guards to escort all visitors—and civilians—off the post, and the soldiers were called to, were summoned to their companies. And it was then that I learned that Pearl Harbor had been attacked. So, it was from there to the radio where I was glued from that time on, because the early news was very disastrous. And there was some doubt in my mind that we could recover from the strikes so devastating. And I remember President Roosevelt getting on and giving his famous speech about the infamous attack and further that we had nothing to fear but fear itself. But I think that was generally the air around my neighborhood. Surprise and disbelief. Because we thought according to what we had been hearing in the news—just casually—that our relationship with Japan was pretty good. And I understand that we were shipping quite a bit of scrap metal to them. We were surprised and shocked.

Denman: Did very many of the young men around you decide they wanted to join up and go fight? Was there any of that in your neighborhood?

Inniss: There was none of that in my neighborhood. We didn't see how we would be directly affected by what had gone on. We knew it was something terrible, but we didn't know that it would impact our lives in the way that we finally learned that it would. But, no, there was not that anxiety, you know, to jump into the fight and do what you could to help save the . . . there was none of that in the neighborhood. We did have some of the young men who had already gone into service, but I don't think they did it with the idea of fighting for their country. I think it was more of a way of surviving.

Denman: Now you were inducted in '43, and you told me earlier that you'd just been married for how long?

Inniss: About four months. About four months. I had been warned. I knew it was coming because when I was married in February of '43, yes, yes. In February of '43, I was working at Flintkote Roofing Company, and I was very displeased with the fact that I was there because we worked swing shift—no differential in pay for night or day work—and the base pay was 53 cents an hour. And there had opened a shipyard called Higgins Shipyard where the men worked in the day for 63 cents an hour and they got a 10 percent differential for working at night. So, I went to this shipyard to apply for a job, and I was told that all I needed to do was get a release from the company where I was working. So I went to the personnel office where I was working at Flintco, asked for a release, and I was told there was no such animal because this is an essential industry, and all personnel are frozen in the jobs here. And the only way you could get a release is to appeal to the War Manpower Commission, and I decided to do that. And, I was asked, "What is your classification?" I said, "One-A." Then I was told, "Why are you so concerned? You're not going to be around very much longer, [laughing]. You know, you're about to be off." And that was a blow to my ego because I thought I'd get a chance to make a little money before I was called off anyway. So, that February that I got married and then June I was inducted into the service.

Denman: You were talking earlier about boot camp experience, about where you went. Could you talk about that some more? You didn't stay in the South—you were sent out of the South . . .

Inniss: Right, right. I was inducted at Camp Livingston, and I was only there about a week, and then shipped off to Cheyenne, Wyoming, for Francis E. Warren, and it was very different because of the elevation—maybe 1,000 feet above sea level—coming from below sea level area. And it was exhausting even to walk, you know, to try to breathe. It was almost a constant nosebleed, you know. And I was one of a few people—I think when we went to Francis E. Warren from Livingston, only five of us were together. We were on a troop train, yes but going to that point, only five of us were discharged so that we were very strange to that atmosphere.

Denman: And you said that there was a very small number of African Americans in Wyoming.

Inniss: Very small number. At Fort Francis E. Warren, out of about sixteen regiments, I'd say there was a battalion of black troops. Although the whole Fort Francis E. Warren was considered replacement training center. It was not a quartermaster headquarters, it was a replacement training center. So that all training initially was infantry training, all training at Fort Francis E. Warren. That was quite a blow, too, because this is my first time in the mountains—you know not walking on flat ground. It's either up a hill or down a hill. And that was challenging. But after I became acclimatized, so to speak, I enjoyed it—the ruggedness of the terrain. It was beautiful. And I didn't encounter anything that I couldn't handle in the way of physical performances. I enjoyed it.

Denman: Now the Army was segregated, weren't you in segregated barracks?

Inniss: Very much so. The Army was segregated and the disappointing . . . well, I was accustomed to segregation. Big deal, you know. So, what else is new? But I did not expect that in the black company, the commissioned officers would be white. This was a shock to me. We're all black, you know, and it took some time to get accustomed to that. Although, I must admit that some of the officers in my company were very professional. Beyond that, maybe even very compassionate. And we were not subjected to any kind of abuse because of the race from the officers who were serving with us. I must admit, at the same time that some of them who had just came out of Officer's Candidate School had hopes of being more productive in the execution of the war. They hoped to have combat activities. And, I think that they knew that that possibility was limited if there were to work with the black soldiers. But, it might have been personal disappointment to some of them, but they didn't show it.

Denman: So do you think that most of your officers were from northern states versus southerners? Was that your impression?

Inniss: That was my impression. That was my impression. I think there was one southerner from Kentucky who was second lieutenant, and I think, Jewish [laughing]. But we got along famously. He was a good soldier, and you couldn't distinguish him from a regular Army person.

Denman: You were saying, on the post, then—even though it was segregated and you had white officers—at least there didn't seem to be some of that tension, and folks got along pretty well? Is that what you're saying?

Inniss: Folks got along very well.

Denman: It's when you went into town that you had problems.

Inniss: When we went to town we had problems because there was no control over civilian policies or practices. And after the conflict had flared up into a riot . . .

Denman: Let's back-track.

Inniss: We want to back track?

Denman: Yeah, because tell me about that. Because at first you said the post was right in Cheyenne.

Inniss: Yes, the post was in Cheyenne.

Denman: There was one black family, right?

Inniss: One black family. You opened the gates of the post at Francis E. Warren and you were in Cheyenne. There was, in Cheyenne, one legitimate black family, and it was headed by our chaplain. We did have a black chaplain. And we had a USO that was, as you would imagine, very much overcrowded. Because we didn't need a pass to, as long as it was after retreat, we could go into Cheyenne at any time. You know, so there was just free access to the City of Cheyenne. There was a USO that was always overcrowded with integrated black and white soldiers together. And we lived in harmony with each other, we fought for the ping-pong table or whatever, but that was always a friendly fight. And I think that some of them sympathized with the fact that we didn't have other outlets that were available to them. Because, as I mentioned, the restaurants, the bars, the theaters, did not cater to the black clientele. And they did surreptitiously. They didn't announce that they didn't want you there, but you just didn't get the service if indeed you were served, it was after a long delay. You understood what was going on. We didn't complain too much about that because we could get occasional weekend passes to Denver. Denver was about 105 miles away and well, Denver was Denver. No, I don't boast of the integration of places in Denver, but there was as larger black community that afforded more things for blacks to do. And incidentally, I must admit that we were served in many of the public places with no embarrassment at all. But that was because there was only a few, comparatively few, black soldiers, in Cheyenne. And I don't know the reason for it, but it became necessary, it seemed for them to bring in—for the camp directors or whoever is in charge of things like this— to bring in more black soldiers to be trained and retrained at Fort Francis E. Warren. And I remember that some of the men to be retrained were tank corpsmen who were coming from Fort Hood, Texas. And they had vibes that they were no longer going to be than corpsmen, and they saw some of that and what was to happen to them thereafter was to be something less prestigious than being a tank corpsman. So that they came in with, let's say, a chip on their shoulder. They were disappointed, yes. And they came in large numbers. Let's say the . . . I hesitate . . . Let's say the number of black troops increased three fold. And they came from Texas Fort Hood—and I don't know what the conditions were in the area where they served, they were greatly displeased with the fact that in Cheyenne there was racial segregation in the public places. So they forced their way into the housing. They forced their way into the restaurants and the bars. And a faction developed. And later on a full-fledged conflagration into a riot. And there was enough blame to be placed on both sides, you know.

Denman: Now when you say riot, what do you mean?

Inniss: When I say riot, I mean fighting with bricks and bottles, and then . . . not with guns.

Denman: Do you think it was started by the servicemen or by the civilians?

Inniss: Well, there was enough blame to go around. Because you heard stories from both sides, and you always had to weigh them, you know, very carefully. I know how we were treated. And this was sometimes hurtful enough to make you angry enough to lash out. But I can't . . . We survived, by not lashing out, you know. We said, "Well, we'll let them have it their way, and then we'll go another way." When it was convenient for us to do so. As long as we once in a while get to Denver, we were happy to go to the USO when we were in Cheyenne, or to stay at the service club when we were on the base. Life was very pleasant. So, I think that the servicemen precipitated the uprising.

Denman: How large was this riot? Are we talking a couple hundred? A couple thousand people?

Inniss: We're talking about a couple hundred people because from the provost marshal came a request to the post commander for additional MPs to help quell the riot. And these MPs came in from Omaha, Nebraska. They had to be imported, MPs from . . . along with the local authorities who didn't seem to have the situation at all in hand. So the military took over, as a matter of fact, to quell the upheaval. Also, just immediately ordered back to camp. No Questions asked. All soldiers to report back to camp and all soldiers were to report to the brigade. The area of the brigade—the jail.

Denman: Everybody?

Inniss: Everybody. Regardless.

Denman: Even if you are down on post or not?

Inniss: Yes. No, no, no. Everybody who is coming in from the town. Whether you are escorted by an MP or not.

Denman: So where were you in all this?

Inniss: I was downtown (laughing). I was downtown and somewhat above the fray because I think that my activities centered primarily around the USO. I liked to play cards; I liked to play ping-pong or to bowl. If I could do that I was happy. Or even sometimes just sit down and, you know, visit with the soldiers from other companies: so no. I was not involved in the actual fighting, but I was there on the scene.

Denman: So you were one of the ones who had to go to the brigade?

Inniss: Yes, I was escorted back to the jail. And when we had been assembled now, obviously it was a small place. They couldn't incarcerate us in the building, so we assembled on the grounds just outside. A large number of soldiers— black and white, incidentally. And I understand there was some fighting on the part of the white soldiers against the white community once they discovered that soldiers were involved. There tended to be a coming together of soldiers no matter the color. So it was soldiers against civilians. And the MPs who came in were black, they were white, and they didn't discriminate. You know, you're just here and you don't go back, do it at once on orders or we were driven back in trucks. When we got there, the post commander addressed us briefly. And said how deplorable the situation had been. And we were then confined to the post, you know, we were not thereafter free to go and come in Cheyenne at will. And the next day, the post commander apologized to the mayor of Cheyenne with the stipulation that he well understood why the thing got started. He said because Cheyenne is not the place for black soldiers. So, in doing that, he appeased the civilian population with an apology, and he also attempted to keep peace on the post by saying that he understood that there was a problem because now that the black population on the post had increased to such numbers, that it was bound something ugly was about to happen. Thereafter, there was tension, but very little relaxing of restraints. I mean, in places where you had not been wanted, you were still not wanted. But some—a few—places said that they were big enough to open up and they would provide service. Especially theaters. They said that they would open their doors and they were sorry that they were contributors to the inhospitable treatment of Negro troops.

Part 3

It Was a Time for . . . Flag Waving

During World War II, patriotism hit an all-time high. It overrode political, ethnic, gender, and status differences. Except for a few profiteers looking to make a quick buck at the expense of others, our home front was functioning like a well-oiled machine. Like it or not, demand for products necessary to win the war took precedence, and items once taken for granted were now unavailable to civilians.

Today, the war on terrorism demands insignificant daily sacrifice from the home front. Even the expression of patriotism itself is regarded by some as "corny," embarrassing, or altogether better forgotten. The same attitude seems to prevail with our National Anthem. How frequently does the American flag fly proudly in front of our homes?

Movie star Jean Arthur standing with escort MP Sergeant William L. Tullo outside of a USO camp show in 1944. [Courtesy Angela A. Tullo]

Wartime Housewife/Mother of Martha Stewart

Martha Kostyra, Connecticut

Yes, I'm Martha Stewart's mother, and yes, I'm very proud of her just as I am proud of all my six children, Eric, Laura, Martha, Frank, Kathryn, and George. Martha and Eric were born during the World War II years, but too young to remember much of those challenging times. There were shortages of everything including food, and I loved to cook so I had to innovate, substitute, and do without like everyone else. There was one exception in that regard because my husband's uncle was a butcher and that did help a little bit.

As a family, we did the usual patriotic things like growing a "victory garden," where much of our food came from. We lived in a very close-knit neighborhood, and would all compete to see who could grow the largest tomatoes, or squash, or whatever . . . it was fun! A very nice retired baker, with the odd name of Mouse, lived nearby and, believe it or not, taught me how to bake. It probably put me on the road to being a darn good cook . . . according to my kids anyhow.

In 1937 I married Edward Kostyra. We lived in Jersey City, New Jersey, and I remember on Pearl Harbor Day in December 1941, we were on our way home from visiting friends in Brooklyn, New York. We saw cars pulled to the curb, and people gathered around talking, and some crying. When we got home, on went the radio, and we learned that the Japanese had bombed our Naval base in Hawaii and that war was declared. It numbed everyone, but we knew we had to get on with our lives and win the battle at home and overseas.

In 1944 our little family moved to Nutley, New Jersey, where Ed worked on building Navy destroyers in the Kearney Shipyards. I guess my role, like so many others, was to keep the home fires burning as an old song goes. My mother was very active with the Red Cross, and my brother and brother-in-law were in the service. My husband had two young cousins, Stefan and Stanley, living with their family in Poland during the outbreak of war. They were American citizens, so decided to escape the Russian invasion, and come to America to enlist in the Air Force and fight for their country. We were deeply touched when after

Little Martha Stewart with mother Martha Kostyra in Jersey City, N.J. c. 1943–44. [Courtesy Martha Kostyra]

Another Jersey City outing including baby Martha Stewart with big brother Eric and relative Stanley Akielaszek, who sadly was a casualty in a training mission. [Courtesy Martha Kostyra]

their harrowing escape from Europe, to learn that Stanley had been killed on a training mission in Council Bluffs, Iowa. Stefan, however, survived and became a translator for the Army in Paris, France, during the liberation. Sooner or later it seemed everyone was personally affected by the tragedy of war!

I remember the contrast of sadness on Pearl Harbor Day, and the great joy on V.J. Day when World War II was ended after four long years. The entire neighborhood on Elm Place gathered together and celebrated for most of the night on V.J. Day. It was almost as unforgettable as the event that caused it in the first place, but not really.

War Bond Tour with Jack Dempsey, Boxing Champ

Marion McManus, Connecticut

"I was born Marion Mabee on May 5, 1909 in Galesburgh, Illinois (just south of Chicago). I may have forgotten a number of things from my past, but not Pearl Harbor Day in 1941."

I was working at the NBC radio studios in New York City as a singer. Some people may remember a show called "Manhattan Merry-Go-Round" which aired every Sunday night between 9:30–10:00. Sunday, March 2, 1941 was my first show, and I stayed for 10 years until television came in and put us off the air, and then I went on to perform other musical theater engagements. Prior to all that, I sang the soprano role in *Carmen* with Nelson Eddy at the Hollywood Bowl, and do you know, at that time they had no mikes in the Bowl. You really had to stretch your tonsils.

When President Franklin D. Roosevelt made his famous "infamy" address to Congress in December 1941 declaring war on Japan and Germany, everyone went crazy! We cried, we were angry, we swore revenge to the enemy, men rushed to join the armed services immediately, other civilians volunteered their time for whatever cause was needed.

At any rate, an entertainment publicist friend got me invited to go on a Government War Bond selling tour with several Fred Waring singers and the great heavyweight boxer Jack Dempsey. He was a nice gentleman. We went first to Richmond, Virginia, where the *USS Token* (a Navy minesweeper) was moored, and went aboard to entertain the crew. It was quite an experience.

By comparison, I sacrificed very little for the World War II cause. Other well-known civilians like actress Carole Lombard suffered tragedies such as being killed in an air crash while on a War Bond tour. Then there were many actors and sports figures who volunteered to entertain our troops anywhere in the world! Well, I did what I could and I'm glad."

For Marion, a show business career was just a matter of time. Her folks moved from Illinois to California in 1920s, where she grew up and went to school with a little girl named Jane Peters, better known as Carole Lombard. Actress Loretta Young lived nearby, so she was influenced by show business families at an early age.

When of age, Marion hopped on a train and headed for New York City. In the 1930s it was *the* place to be for a budding singer. She was overwhelmed by the skyscrapers, giants compared to the maximum 12-story buildings in Los Angeles. After several struggling years she managed to find a theatrical agent, rented an apartment, and her career began to take off. By that time she had married her first husband,

Marion McManus with Coast Guard Commander Jack Demsey (World Heavyweight Champion 1919–26) headed to a War Bond Rally. [Courtesy Marion McManus]

George McManus, a Naval Observer for President Roosevelt. Then came Pearl Harbor! "George was on a mission for the President in a remote area called Sierra Leone in Africa, and you can believe," says Marion, "that as a newly married girl my thoughts and prayers were with him, first and foremost on Pearl Harbor Day."

So goes the Marion McManus story . . . just a segment from another woman who lived through, and contributed to the World War II home front effort!

A Fighter to Be Reckoned With

Justin Barzda, Connecticut

"Can one fall in love with an airplane? Absolutely—if it's the F4U-1. The day I saw a rendering of this new fighting aircraft, I had to become a part of it. From its pictures and publicity, to me the Corsair appeared the epitome of design and performance. The first time I climbed into the Corsair cockpit, I felt I was sitting on the edge of a cliff. The cockpit floor was the bottom of the fuselage, about 3 feet below the seat and rudder pedal troughs. I surmise early military pilots were also uncomfortable. If they dropped anything, it was gone for the mission.

On October 1, 1941, I was gratified to be employed by Vought-Sikorsky, since I viewed the gull-winged Corsair (aptly named) as a superior fighting machine. It was exciting to know that I would be part of designing and creating this Navy fighter with its advanced high-speed performance and rugged fighting power. After a stint in the Change Group, getting indoctrinated in their systems and procedures, I was assigned to the control design group where I began my apprenticeship in design of control system parts and runs throughout the aircraft. The F4U-1 was in the final stage of production design.

Much of my time was involved in the design of experimental and production "tab" controls for the moveable aileron, elevator, and rudder control services. Experimental systems demonstrated the principles and confirmed results. Production systems were then incorporated into production line aircraft. The simplest was the "trim" tab which could be set by the pilot to balance out aircraft flight longitudinal and/or lateral imbalances, thus reducing his control stick force, conserving energy for more important mission duties.

Two other types of tabs were "leading" and "spring" tab controls. The leading tab moved in a set ratio to the angular displacement of the control surface and created a force to move the control surface in the direction desired by the pilot, reducing his control stick force.

But at higher speeds, the relief force could become excessive and may let the pilot get in dangerous maneuver situations. Thus the introduction of the "spring" tab system. The tab moves only in proportion to the control system loads; greater angles at higher speeds, reducing pilot control stick forces. The goal was to give the pilot a uniform feel and a response for all conditions of flight. A design challenge was to combine some of these systems to simplify controls. Another endeavor was to finalize the production design of a "master" control which would properly activate and set flap, landing gear, arresting hook controls for a ground or aircraft landing according to the pilot's wish. One lever for multiple functions.

One of the early modifications was a redesign of the cockpit arrangement to include a floor. I did the redesign basic layout of structural, seating, and flight and engine control arrangements. This was tweaked with mockup and layout consultations with other engineering specialists and pilots. When the Corsair needed design modifications indicated by "Service" use, they were essentially completed. I moved on to other aircraft projects and preliminary design. Since the Navy's initial purchase of 584 of the Corsair in 1941, over the years that figure grew to more than 12,500 F4U models.

When I gazed outside the engineering department windows, I was able to distinguish who was flying the Corsair—chief test pilot, experimental test pilot, production pilots or service delivery airmen—by the steepness of their take off and landing patterns. I remember fondly that the "slick" looking plane was considered one of WWII's greatest fighter planes. It could outfight, out climb, and (if need be) outrun any prop-driven enemy, especially Japan's Zero. How exciting it was to see hundreds of Corsairs come off the assembly line, and thrilling to learn that these war birds would soon be on their way to the South Pacific theatre of operations!!

The Corsair ... Lean and Mean

Lee DiBattista, Connecticut

Here are the best recollections I have of the Chance Vought gull-winged Corsair aircraft. As a mad supporter of the propeller-driven Corsair as being the best fighter aircraft of World War II vintage, I contest all who would claim otherwise. This is my opinion as an engineer involved in the design components of same.

During the war the original Corsair design was updated and changed four times, the most drastic revision was made as a result of a dire need for fighter bombers, especially in the Pacific theatre to fight the Japanese. Called the F4U-Corsair, its capabilities were astonishing compared to its peers.

This new demand for fighter bombers brought severe pressure on all the engineering resources of Vought. Every person involved was on unlimited overtime. I was involved and I remember we were allowed to sleep in the Company's fire department cots, so we could work longer hours. A new model Pratt & Whitney engine was installed to increase the horse power to 2,400; but the most important changes were the design hardware additions, permitting the aircraft to carry two 500-pound bombs under its gull wing (one on each side), or a 1,000-pound bomb on its center line, or an alternative 250-gallon droppable fuel tank and increasing its fire power from six 50-caliber machine guns to four 20-millimeter cannons—a very necessary strafing advantage. This permitted an extension of range, giving the Marines a fighter bomber to support General MacArthur's ground campaign in the Pacific.

I remember clearly in July 1944 the quota of Corsairs was met for the month . . . meaning 13 aircraft per day! Chance Vought won the U.S. Navy "E" award. Thirteen thousand persons were employed at this high point, three shifts a day, seven days a week. During a first month of the F4U-4 production a critical engine control part from another source held up delivery of aircraft resulting in a stack-up of Corsairs which used every bit of land available at the Bridgeport Airport. There were aircraft everywhere, in the fields, the courtyards, parking lots. When the missing part was installed and delivery began, the Navy would fly in their twenty-three pilots in a D.C. transport. The best they could do was move out two squadrons daily. It took the better part of two weeks to deliver all the aircraft.

Corsair combat was so interesting that another unusual occurrence took place in the 1970s when a TV program ran for several years covering the exploits in the South Pacific of the Corsair and pilots called "The Black Sheep Squadron." They were led by the daring air ace Gregory "Pappy" Boyington and he was portrayed by actor Robert Conrad.

As I purge my memory I recall other items germane to the period, and the most remarkable Corsair fighter/bomber used so valiantly by our U.S. Navy fighter pilots during WWII. But, I must stop somewhere. I am thankful for the opportunity of having been part of its history.

Courtesy Lee DiBattista

Navy WAVE Pharmacist Mate

Anne Cole-Beers, Connecticut

I was born in Beverly, Massachusetts, and grew up in Winchester, Massachusetts, a small New England town 12 miles north of Boston. I was the youngest of three children with very vivid memories of the war years.

Every Saturday afternoon during the 1938–1940 when I was 14 to 16 years old, we went to the movie downtown. Before each movie there was a 10–15 minute news reel (all black and white) of Hitler and the war in Europe. All we saw was Gestapo youth goose-stepping, and swastikas and bombs, and ruins in Poland, France, etc. It made a tremendous impression on all of us high school kids. My older brother was in a military prep school, and my Dad had been in the Army in France in WWI, so our family with a history dating back to the *Mayflower* was all very patriotic.

December 7, 1941, I can still vividly remember I was home from school, and standing in the kitchen listening to the radio. Suddenly, my music program was interrupted with the horrendous news about "the Japs" attack on Pearl Harbor. Everyone was in shock! President Roosevelt declared war, and in no time it seemed the draft was in operation.

Everyone wanted to help. We were mad as hell at the Japanese and at Hitler as well. The draft took boys at 18 years old, but girls had to be 20, with their parents' permission—and girls were not drafted. They were strictly volunteers. My brother, Don, however, went to the Army immediately, but my sister and I were too young to join.

That summer, 1942, my friend and I applied for jobs at the General Electric plant in Lynn, Massachusetts. The men had gone to war, and women had to take over their jobs. The G.E. plant made airplane parts, and we were trained to be welders. We were on the 7–3 shift. We got up at 5:30, drove to work, wore helmets with face guards to protect our faces from flying particles of metal. We worked with many tough women and got razzed for being college kids, but we learned a lot and felt we were helping.

During that summer of 1942 life was suddenly different. We were at our summer home in Marblehead, Massachusetts, on the Atlantic Ocean about 20 miles north of Boston. The entire east coastline was blacked-out at sundown. Our windows were covered, there were no street lights, and the Coast Guard air station across the harbor from our house had training planes and scouting/search planes taking off and landing constantly (sea planes, of course).

Every four hours, two sailors in uniform walked through our back yard patrolling the waterfront. On my day off, my sister and I would be sunning on chaises directly in line with where the guys walked.

Pharmacist Mate 3rd class Anne Cole-Beers while on leave as a Navy WAVE (WAVES: Women Accepted for Volunteer Emergency Service) during the early 1940s. [Courtesy Anne Cole-Beers]

Remember, they were 18 to 19 years old and so cute in their uniforms we instantly became friends!

By 1943, my brother was a 1st Lieutenant in the Army, and my sister had enlisted in the Marine Corps as soon as she turned 20. I was still too young, but in June of 1944 I left Tufts University to enlist in the Navy WAVES. I went to Hunter College in NYC for basic training, then to Bethesda Naval Hospital in Virginia for permanent duty. I had chosen to be a Pharmacist Mate in the Hospital Corps, because as a psychology major at Tufts, I wanted to work with sailors injured physically and emotionally.

The Pacific War was in full swing. The casualties were high, and the Portsmouth Naval Hospital was noted for treating burn cases. We had trains arriving from California in the middle of the night with burn victims from Iwo Jima and other Pacific Battles. It was our job to rehabilitate them. I can remember being in full uniform and standing at attention with music playing as the stretchers were unloaded and the guys were carried into the ward. We were all about the same age, so we bonded immediately. I met guys from all over the U.S. I had to give them back rubs and shots for my night-time duty, and in the daytime I helped run the Occupational Therapy program to help them get back on their feet and forget their horrendous experiences in the South Pacific. They kidded with us constantly about "relieving a man for active duty"!!

We laughed a lot, we cried a lot, but it was an experience I would reflect on my whole life. I made wonderful friends I'm still in touch with, one from Oklahoma and one from Wisconsin were my best friends. I fell in love with a Marine patient on the base. He was from South Carolina. I wonder where he is now!

Our quarters were cubicles in a big dorm with two sets of bunk beds, four to a cubicle. We had night duty several times a month and sometimes twice. I remember vividly I had to sit a watch where the patient died. It was so sad. These were all young men who fought for their country.

My Mom and Dad had a big flag outside our home showing three kids enlisted, 1 Army, 1 Navy, 1 Marine. Boy, were they proud of us! My brother was an officer but my sister and I were enlisted so we had to salute him.

The war ended in August 1945 and I was mustered out in June of 1946. I went back to Tufts for my senior year, after serving twenty months, and graduated with honors in June of 1947.

USO Volunteer . . . Dramatic Experiences

Vivian van Allen, Oregon

It was my wedding day, September 1, 1939, and Hitler has just attacked Poland. My heavenly day had been planned for the Friday of Labor Day weekend because it was the only honeymoon we could afford. My mother awakened me early that morning with word that war had broken out. My then fiancé and I had agreed that if something threatening happened, we would be married quickly.

Each day was a nightmare waiting to happen as we wondered if Ben, my husband, would be drafted. Our marriage kept him off the head of the line, but we had no children tying him down. Also, he was in the insurance business and that line of work was nothing critical to hold a man back. By the age of 29, at the time of Pearl Harbor, he was not a prime suspect for the draft.

December 7th, we were driving home from church, listening to the radio, when we heard the heart-stopping announcement. The country had been building up to this and instantly, everything changed. Ben continued to work all day and came home to sleep in the evening. Classes were offered at night for those interested in working for the war, and around midnight Ben would get up to attend a class in sheet metal work.

When my husband was inevitably shipped overseas, we worked out a code to use in our letters. "Darling" would mean England. "Sweetheart" was the Pacific. The last codeword we used was "Beloved" and that was North Africa. It was not uncommon for people to use such codes to get around the censors.

After he left, I went back to Portland for work. My assignment was as a hostess in the lounge, which was located next door to the railroad station. I greeted people as they came in for all sorts of reasons. Some came in to sit at the stations specifically for writing letters. Others came to sleep in the bunked rooms. There was a record player in good condition that often played, but no one ever came to dance.

Nearby, there was also a canteen that the USO sponsored. On occasion I would fill in there, especially as the war continued on. It was so intriguing how the men that came back only wanted milk, milk, milk. One gentleman that came in asked for five glasses right in front of him, all at once.

I can remember one awful night when a WAVE, a female in the Navy, came in very distraught. She was young, unmarried, and knew that she was having a miscarriage. She desperately did not want the Navy to find out about it and she was in dire need of medical attention. I took her into the bunk room and let her lie down there. She begged me not to let the Navy know. There was not a thing I could do otherwise, though. We had certain directives and in case of any emergency with part of the Service, we had to contact that specific Service. We had no authority to go outside of it. It was the hardest thing to make the call against her wishes.

Somebody from the Navy came to get her, but I have no idea what happened to her afterward. That was difficult to deal with. I would often make these bonds with people, even if only for ten minutes, but then they would leave and I would never hear from them again. I did not get the opportunity to learn if they were all right.

It brings chills down my spine when I recall an incident that took place after the war in the Pacific ended. The first men to come back were the prisoners, our men who had been prisoners of the Japanese. They were immediately sent to Hawaii for a month of medical evaluation, treatment, and feeding. Once they were noticeably healthier, they were sent to hospitals near their homes. One night when I was down there, we asked to go out to a certain train track and split up. Each of us was to go to a different car to talk with these men. They were all in bed and still very thin and weak. Our discussions were a matter of answering questions they might have on a number of topics. They were starving for any information they could find out about home. What nearly finished me was this one man in particular who leaned over when there was a break in the conversation to ask if I had anything to do with a "Dear John" letter. He had come back to one saying, "I found somebody else." We did not go into details, but I suppose the woman was already married to the other man.

Those were two of the most dramatic times, but otherwise, I found this time of my life to be an exceedingly worthwhile and very fulfilling time. Some of the prettiest music came out of World War II. The spirit was so pervasive and everyone had it. It was ubiquitous and everyone felt it, especially since the war was over and our country was together . . . and free once again.

My Postwar Experience

Del Markoff, Connecticut

Looking back at the time of my life when I finished almost four and one-half years in the army, and found myself once more a civilian, brings both moments of sadness and feelings of excitement and relief. How to explain this mysterious mélange of life at that time and the perspective of history just passed?

My final station when the war ended in August 1945 was at Wright-Patterson Field in Ohio. A separation center was opened there in September, and based on the points I had accumulated I was among the first officers to be released. In June 1941, I was a healthy young bachelor, and by now I had met and married Adele Bloch, and was the father of two boys, about to take on the responsibilities of the head of a family in a totally different world. The times were spectacular for me. To think, first of all, of my fortunate position, I returned whole, having not been a statistic of over 1 million casualties including 300,000 deaths during the war. I was ready, willing, and able to make a whole new life for myself and my family.

In retrospect, I was deprived of one of my most fervent pre-war wishes—to become a tax lawyer. My law class never finished (it was about to now). But now with a family to support I had a most fortunate alternative—a position awaiting me in a successful family business manufacturing table and floor lamps for national distribution. Besides the change from military to civilian life, the everyday living world had a new environment. No more rationing, no more price controls. Millions of young men about to be re-absorbed into a country that had been so regimented and dedicated entirely to the defeat of its enemies.

I found myself back in Chicago, where I was born and raised. Fortunately, when rent controls were abrogated by President Truman, Chicago went along (whereas, for example, New York did not). While there were problems in finding a place to live, this was a temporary situation. The building industry got into gear and within a few years there was a sufficiency of apartments in the city to make choices (New York City by contrast had a perpetual shortage). Business went into an instant expansion mode to make up for consumer goods shortages that were brought on by the needs of war. My family business prospered as did so many others.

My life was great. How lucky I was! At the same time for so many others new opportunities presented themselves that because of the war and its aftermath, simply could not have existed pre-war. The GI Bill of Rights created education opportunities for a whole generation that contributed mightily to our national recovery. While I did not benefit from this personally, my life was much improved by the economic and social environment that was created. Yes, it was a great time in my life. But it was a great time for my country. How fortunate to have been an American at that time. I smile every time I think of the halcyon days of 1945 to 1949!

Working Together in a Time of War

Mary Kowalsky, Connecticut

When I heard the radio broadcast telling the world about the bombing of Pearl Harbor, I started to cry. I was on my way home from high school and watched solemnly as cars stopped by the side of the road, listening to the news. People were hugging each other and crying, also. There were no strangers in that moment in time. We were all Americans. It was unbelievable.

The second I reached my house, I ran in and called to my mother who had just heard the news. "It's going to be bad," I remember gasping to her. And it was.

Reality sunk in that America really was at war and instantly, dozens of programs sprung up. I especially remember "Bundles for Britain," an effort to aid our foreign friends who had entered the war sooner than we had. Anyone who could knit was asked to help make scarves, mittens, and sweaters to send to the soldiers. I wanted to do my part so I joined a group session to learn how to make gloves. I received a pattern to make a right-handed glove, but at the time I did not realize that to make a left-hand you had to reverse the instructions. For that reason, I just kept making right-handed gloves over and over again. It amused me to wonder if there was another "dummy" like me out there who only knew how to make left-handed gloves.

After school ended for the afternoon, my fellow high school students and I would gather to roll bandages for the American Red Cross. People donated clean sheets and our job was to cut them into strips and turn them into bandages for the wounded. We made rolls of all sizes and packed them in groups of 100 for shipping overseas.

Being a senior in high school, I was old enough to become an Assistant Air Raid Warden. Another obligation of the townspeople was to have black-out curtains installed in their homes so that no light could show through if an enemy attacked. My duty as an AARW was to go out each night and check for light peeping through the windows. If any was seen, even the tiniest speck, I had to knock on the door and tell the owners they must black it out. Many protested they had done enough already, but I still had to make them put in an extra strip to leave no corner exposed. Another task was to make sure that those walking at night did not carry lanterns or flashlights. At a far distance, even those small lights could be seen from the air.

Food was rationed and we all had food stamps. Housewives saved fat from the meat and that was used to make ammunition and explosives. I never understood how it worked or why, but we saved it religiously. My family even used the fat to make our own soap. We added lye to it and though it was not the best substance for our skin, it kept us clean.

Many of my friends, my very young friends, were enlisting in the armed services. They were only 18 or 19 years old, but were drafted nonetheless. Seven boys from the neighborhood enlisted, along with my brother. Thankfully, he was rejected because later on news came back that all seven boys were killed in action. Those who lost their sons in battle placed gold stars in their windows and respectively called themselves "Gold Star Mothers." As the war progressed, it became more and more common to pass by windows decorated to honor lost sons.

My mother used to cry every night and refused to let me work in a factory even though I was old enough. She, like other women, wore dark-colored clothing every day because lighter colors would reflect light and everyone feared an air attack. Thankfully, it never came, but still, there was not much color in our life as a result.

In my hometown, the townspeople set up a hospital in the Town Hall. They brought in victims after they were released from service and were in dire need of medical assistance. I decided to help and took a course in Home Nursing and Red Cross First Aid. We used ketchup as blood in our training classes and I remember my mother being so upset over it because ketchup was scarce and she thought it was a terrible waste.

I remember the Bond Rallies and the Great entertainment that would come into town. Everyone would attend the concerts and buy bonds to support the war effort. A person could only attend the Bond Rally if he bought at least $100 in bonds. Marion Anderson even came to sing at a concert. At the time, I was friendly with the manager and he asked me to hold Marion's mink coat while she sang. I never forgot that night.

I also never forgot how fortunate my family was during these times. We raised chickens and cows and always had milk and eggs, which were both scarce. My mother used to buy a special kind of water and fill glass containers with it to store the eggs all winter long. To preserve food, all the women would congregate for canning parties. They canned jellies, pickles, apples, tomatoes, and whatever they could. Nothing went to waste and what one family could not use, they shared with another. It was a hard time, but the American people worked to- gether to get through it. In some ways, it was an unforgettable time. People were warmer to their neighbors and everyone was concerned about everyone else. I never would have thought people would be closer, kinder, and so selfless as a result of our country being attacked and our men being shipped away, but I guess . . . the war makes you that way.

Key West, Florida, 1941

Armer White, Florida

Prior to the beginning of World War II, I was working for Florida Power and Light Company as a salesman. I was 28 years old and had two boys. My third son was born in March of 1942, a short time after the start of the war. They were all born in room 25—Victoria Hospital. An interesting aspect on this particular subject is the cost of bringing children into the world now as opposed to the cost in the 1930s and early '40s. My son Armer, Jr.'s cost was $30 for three days in the hospital including the delivery room. The doctor charged $25. So it cost $55 to bring him into the world.

Like all other able-bodied men, I had to register for the draft. However, when Pearl Harbor occurred in December of 1941, I was already involved in defense work. Actually, I was employed by Mackle-Leach Construction Co. as an office manager and purchasing agent.

I had actually been in Key West for several days when we learned of the tragedy of Pearl Harbor. Within a few days after the U.S. declared war, the company received an emergency order to start major reworking of the submarine pens, which had sadly deteriorated since they were built during World War I. We then negotiated a contract to build a major section base, which consisted of building houses for enlisted men and officers. We also started a major land clearing project for Boca Chica Naval Air Station, which required us to work both day and night for months. Even though I was in very essential work, I applied for a commission in the Seabees, a construction division in the Navy. I could not, however, get a release from the officer in charge of construction to leave the job I was doing in Key West.

My family stayed in Miami, but later on, I sent them back, as living was tough in Key West. Everything was rationed and it was hard to get meat and vegetables. All water had to be boiled because it consisted of rainwater dripping off the roofs, which were stored in concrete cisterns. There was no fresh water in the Keys. It was not until 1943 that a pipeline was built to bring water from Homestead, Florida to Key West. This water line is still bringing water to the Keys.

Almost everything came into the city by trucks. They traveled over narrow wooden bridges on U.S. 1 and at any given moment, they could have easily been destroyed by fire. There was a stream of trucks bringing in everything from lumber to concrete blocks, as well as equipment and personnel on a twenty-four hour basis. Armed personnel was part of every convoy. After the submarine warfare by the Germans was eliminated, we were finally able to ship petroleum.

The Boca Chica Naval Air Station was finished in 1942. They had planes in there using a runway in less than a year, but they were flying in from other air bases. A temporary refueling operation took place there while major fuel storage below ground was under construction. Submarine warfare was taking a terrible toll on our shipping and the Air Force had to deal with the emergency any way they could. Planes were landing and taking off before we even had below-ground gasoline storage. Above-ground storage in tanks and barrels was the order of the day. As soon as the base was finished, the aircraft went to work on the submarines, which had enjoyed a field day without shipping. They sank ships within sight of Key West day, and night, but they could not deal with the bombs and depth charges that the aircraft unleashed upon them. With the constantly increasing number of planes we were building, submarines were soon being eliminated throughout the whole Atlantic Ocean. In the Key West area, they were eliminated by the end of 1943.

As a rescue service, the Coast Guard had boats that operated all around Key West both in the Atlantic and in the Gulf. They tried in every way possible to minimize the casualties of the torpedoed tankers and freighters. They picked out of the water huge numbers of crews from torpedoed ships. There were a gruesome number of oil-burned casualties in every sinking because most of the stricken ships were tankers. Many of those died before they could be rescued and numbers of bodies were constantly washing ashore in Key West.

The city did its part to aid the war effort and after the war took a definite turn in favor of the Allies, there was no more heavy demand for new construction on bases there or anything else. Actually, the war began to wind down and people started to lead a more normal lifestyle. Everything in the way of consumer goods was still in very short supply, so I took a job as a sales manager in Coral Gables. There I continued until I went into the real estate business. This led to a long association in the development of many new communities in Florida, including Port Charlotte, Port St. Lucie, Spring Hill, and Deltona, among others.

Newspaperman in a World War II Shipyard

Frank S. Hopkins, Florida

"What do you think you're going to do in a shipyard?" the managing editor demanded. He was irritated but also curious.

"It's sort of a personnel and labor relations job," I said.

"But you haven't had that kind of experience," he exploded. "You're a newspaperman!"

"That doesn't mean I can't learn something about industrial relations," I said obstinately.

"But why leave newspaper work?"

"I've got to get into this war somehow. I'd probably be a lousy soldier, but I believe that I could be useful in a war industry," I answered.

He looked unconvinced, but I went on.

"At least I'm used to mixing with people, and that should be a help."

"You'll find it a lot more complicated than that," he growled.

He didn't know how right he was.

This conversation took place in the newsroom of a nationally known newspaper in June 1941. I was 33 years old, and had been in journalistic work of one sort or another ever since my college days. Going into industry was certainly a new departure for me. But it had been a crazy, upsetting spring. The Germans had taken Yugoslavia, Greece, and Crete, and were threatening the Suez Canal; and even as we talked they were daily plunging deeper into Russia. To anyone with an imagination, it seemed that the whole world was in flames. And yet America would not wake up, would not face the issue.

I was restless, emotionally disturbed, unhappy. I had expected to return to Harvard in the fall of 1941, where a teaching fellowship in sociology had been awarded to me. I was planning graduate studies, and thinking seriously about an academic career. But I knew it was no use—not with a war coming on. I had to do something active. I had been deeply interested in social studies during a Nieman Fellowship year at Harvard two years before, and was aware that many interesting things about human behavior were coming to light in industrial research. Although I was the merest amateur, I thought that in industry my awareness of sociological theory might be helpful.

Putting my plan into effect was astonishingly easy. I got in touch with an acquaintance in industry—a brilliant young industrial relations executive who was about my age—to ask his advice. Almost before I knew it he was negotiating with me to come work in his plant, a ship repair organization which in normal times employed about 1,000 people, but which already had mushroomed to nearly 4,000.

When I went down to look the place over, I almost lost my nerve. The glaring summer sun, beating down on the dirty dry docks, piers, and shops, made the shipyard seem singularly uninviting. At the piers lay shapeless old red hulks with smokestacks and superstructures removed, old World War I ships which had been brought in to be reconditioned for the British under lease-lend. Building materials for new piers and buildings cluttered up the yard. The administration office was old, small, and crowded.

But when I talked with the president, a pleasant, plumpish, pink-faced man in his early forties, it seemed different. Swinging his chair around to get a view of the waterfront, he assured me that the ship repair business, in which he had spent his life, was the most glamorous occupation any man could want. I like people who have a deep emotional feeling about their work. I figured him for a square-shooter, and I was right. My doubts were gone.

Then came the problem of adjusting to the organization. I was to be a general assistant to my industrial relations friend, who at the time was assistant to the president and later on was made a vice president.

"We're going to give you a desk and eventually an office, but God only knows what your duties will be," he told me. "You're to learn everything you can, and do whatever comes along. You can start by sitting in on my meetings with the Union, and I'd like you to see what you can do to help us get our training program underway."

For my first three weeks, I put on overalls and followed one of the production executives around the ships. I met and talked with shipyard people—scores of them. And I formed my first opinion about industry. I quickly became convinced that the people I was learning to know were just as interesting due to the drafting of men into the armed services; the training of women to do men's work in our yard had passed from the experimental stage to that of real necessity. The outlook is for more women, who must be properly introduced into our organization, properly supervised, and properly trained to help us win this war. [Article courtesy of son Richard S. Hopkins]

Part 4

It Was a Time for ...
War-Plant Women

There were many home front skeptics regarding the role women could play as wartime workers. Then came reality and the question: If they did not take over, who would? So these inexperienced women bit the bullet, learned the rules, jumped in feet first—and excelled. The transition was fascinating to witness.

With factories working at top speed twenty-four hours a day, seven days a week, and able-bodied men serving in the armed forces, women and girls took over where men left off. By the thousands they made an about-face, left the security of "homemaker" or went directly from high school into the world of commerce and unexplored territory as bread winners and pioneers in the workplace, determined to do their share for the war effort. Many factory women used muscles they never before knew they had. Some worked on dangerous jobs, but it had to be done—and they did it.

Worker on a lathe in a factory once manufacturing fountain pens, and then converted to producing parts for the war effort. [Courtesy Westport Public Library]

One of many wartime female factory workers using a drill press to assemble parts for use in aircrafts. [Courtesy Westport Public Library]

[National Archives and Records Administration]

[National Archives and Records Administration]

In 1943 a graphic artist, J. Howard Miller, produced this poster for the Westinghouse Corporation. It became the poster girl for "Rosie the Riverter." [National Archives and Records Administration]

Nineteen-Year-Old Depth Charge Factory Worker

Mina Burke, Indiana

At age 19, during WWII, I worked at Stewart Warner, a factory that made depth charges. We were civilian employees of the Navy and worked under Civil Service. Our job was to inspect the parts made and the completed product of the Mark 6, Model 2 Depth Charge and Booster Extenders. I dealt with company stock boys, expeditors, and Navy representatives, and though I was a woman, I never met with difficulties.

I worked on both the assembly line and in the "Cage." On the assembly line, inspection is made according to the model's class. A functional test as well as a leak test is performed on the booster of the depth charge, overseen by the inspector. My part in the testing process was to perform and record the results of the final firing tests under water. One supervisor, I can recall, yelled at me for rejecting a number of charges because they did not fire at the right pressure. He told my direct supervisor that I had no business rejecting the charges. He was partly right. I was only 19, just out of high school. I did not know anything. My ability to read blueprints was solely due to the fact that in the 1930s I made my own clothes and grew a knack for following patterns. It was fairly easy for me to read the blueprints and the air and water pressures. I knew that the charges I rejected were not acceptable and I was right. The Navy Inspector of Engineer Materials backed me up. After that, we did not have many more rejections.

At a later time, my job sent me to a factory that made hospital tents. I would check them for rips and tears, and some were defective. Rather than reject the whole tent as was customary to do, I had the employees sew patches upon the torn spots. When the Navy Brass came to oversee my work, they were impressed and asked where the idea for patching the problem came from. I informed them I was a child brought up in the Depression and we had done similar things to our worn out clothes.

My family also participated in the war effort in their own ways. My mother took classes with the Red Cross in order to become a nurse at Dukes Memorial Hospital. The hospitals needed help and my mother hoped her two hands could make a difference. At night, my father, who only had an eighth-grade education, taught a mechanics class at the local high school. I had two sisters who also were busy aiding our country in its time of need. My older sister worked in a defense plant and my younger sister joined the Cadet Nurse Corps, both in Indiana. I spent my winters in Florida, but in the summer, I always returned to Indiana where they were.

From Civilian Directly to Army WAAC

Anne Breise, Nebraska

"In 1941, I worked in a factory in Chicago that was located midway between her western suburbs and Chicago's Loop. Actually, the physical make-up of that company was composed of two buildings located directly across the street from each other." Fifty-eight years after Anne Breise became part of the war effort, her recollections were as fresh as though the events had happened yesterday.

"The smaller building, although it was anything but small, was made up of two huge rooms. Various machines and inspection tables were kind of all mixed up in those two rooms. I would guess that several hundred employees worked there. Mid-point in those two rooms was a caged-in area referred to as "The Cage." It made up the shop office. Inside was a desk, a table, a couple of chairs, a file cabinet, and a phone. The file contained orders for products made, so we could keep track of how a particular order was being filled. We counted boxes of items made every shift. Upstairs on either side of the first room were locker rooms—one side for men and one side for women. Restrooms were located there along with tables and benches that we could use during our lunch hour. Just about everyone carried a sack lunch. The second large room was very much like the first room—filled with machines and inspection tables." Work assignments seemed to be determined by which skills women or men were thought at the time to do best. "Men ran the machines while women did the inspection work. Various gauges were used to measure depth, circumference, hardness or softness of metal, etc. Women wore three-quarter length smocks to protect their clothes. With the machines running and using deep metal pans to hold the products being made, it was very noisy in that shop."

The change over from peace to war work was not without stress, both industrial and personal. Changes had to be made in the workplace and it took time for adjustment to the new wartime products and regulations. "When we were a factory, we made metal lamp parts and tappets for cars. We ordered parts for the machines through their purchasing agent. After Pearl Harbor was attacked, we became a defense plant almost immediately. No longer did we make metal lamp parts or tappets for cars. Instead, we made tappets for tanks and studs for airplane motors. And where we had been running two shifts of workers for a 45-hour work week, we began running three shifts of workers seven days a week. Members of a workers' union began picketing outside the plant every day in all kinds of weather in an attempt to make ours a union shop. It took a while, but eventually they did succeed, and all jobs were rated for a pay scale."

Anne had a particularly vivid recollection of one person—and for a reason that became personal. "Within 'the cage' was one man with the title of 'Shop-Office-Person.' He noted the progress on our orders in the file, checked on raw stock, saw to it that payroll adjustments were made in the main office, and encouraged employees to sign up for war bonds to be taken out of their salaries. Being a 'Shop-Office-Person' was a cleaner job than running a machine or doing inspection work, but the union rated that job low on the pay scale. Eventually, the man who did that job was called into military service. So, my boss offered me that job. That caused me to be shunned by the other women in my department. They refused to talk to me because they had more seniority than I did, and they felt that one of them should have been offered that job. I remember my boss asking me how I liked my new job after I'd been doing it for about a week. I answered that I didn't know for sure since nobody was speaking to me. He replied, 'they'll get over it,' and they did, but I felt very uncomfortable for the first couple of weeks in that position."

"As the war went on in 1942, most of the younger, physically able men were called into military service. What was left behind were key personnel, physical rejects, and older married men." That led to arrangements that would have been intolerable before the war. "Affairs between young single women and older family men became the subject for gossip. However, many of the foremen and supervisors were never called upon to serve their country through the military. They were long-time employees of the plant and could better serve the war effort by remaining on their jobs. There was no time to train anybody else to know what they already knew. So, key personnel were given military deferments of six months at a time hoping the war would end. When it didn't, they were given another six-month deferment, and that went on throughout the war."

"In early 1943 I left the defense plant to enlist in the Women's Army Auxiliary Corps. While I was in the service, a law was passed that gave all former veterans the right to return to their former jobs once the war ended." But would she want that old job back after the war? "I don't remember how many veterans did do that because I've never seen statistics. I do know that after being in the military service for several years, you go through a period of readjustment once you return to civilian life. Both of my brothers went through that readjustment after they were discharged. One had been in the Navy for four years, and the other had served the Coast Guard for three and a half years. They each tried a number of different jobs before finally settling down. I went through a readjustment period myself, although I didn't realize it at the time. I just knew that I had risen above that defense plant, and I no longer belonged there. That plant did very well with defense contracts. So, not too long after the war ended, they built a brand new plant in the far western suburbs of Chicago. My former boss continued to work there until he retired."

One of the First Women Workers in the Brooklyn Navy Yard

Ida Pollack, New York

The *New York Times* wrote an article about some of my co-workers and me on Monday, September 14, 1942. We were the first women ever to be hired to do mechanical work in a shipyard, the Brooklyn Navy Yard, that is. The company hired us to aid the war effort by filling in for the men who were drafted or volunteered to stop Hitler's drive to take over the world. We became electric arc welders, acetylene gas burners, and ship fetters. We broke a 141-year tradition; they hired 200 of us. We wore slacks and no jewelry.

Shipbuilding and repairs to damaged ships were ongoing around the clock in three ten-hour shifts. Every three months we rotated. Overall, it was a great experience for me even though the hours were long and the work was often very difficult. The girls and I had some fun, and shared in the sense of accomplishment, the sense of satisfaction that we contributed to the defeat of Hitler. As soon as the armistice was signed, though, we were separated from our roles as workers and the shipyard returned to "normal."

"First Women Hired in Navy Yard Shops"
New York Times, September 14, 1942

Women are working as mechanics in the Navy Yard in Brooklyn for the first time in its 141-year history, headquarters of the Third Naval District revealed yesterday. Shop officials said they were much pleased with the first batch of women working there and looking forward to employment of more.

When the United States Civil Service Commission announced that women could take an examination for prospective mechanics, 20,000 applied. Among them were young girls fresh from school or college, women whose husbands were in the armed services, and some professional women. Of the applicants, 6,000 were examined and 3,000 qualified as eligible.

"Thus far, the Navy yard has sent out calls for 200 of these eligible and they are coming in daily. The shopfitters' shop has asked for 100 of that number and expects to ask for more. Other shops, which have no facilities for training so large a number, are asking for smaller groups. The ordinance machine shop expects six to report soon, the foundry has requested five, and the paint shop four.

Rules for working clothes laid down by the labor board bar skirts, loose sleeves, frills, shoes with high heels or open toes, pendant earrings, necklaces, bracelets, and finger rings. The mechanic learners wear coveralls or slacks equipped with flat hip pockets and no cuffs and welding shields, were issued by the shipyard. Caps, hats, or turbans are specified to prevent hair from catching in moving machinery.

The experience of shop supervisors at the Navy yard was said to agree with the findings of executives in other armament plants where women have been engaged to relieve men for combat duty. Women have been found to excel at jobs requiring a high degree of manual dexterity, speed, and accuracy.

They cannot as a class, it was noted, qualify for jobs that require considerable physical strength or for those that necessitate skills that can be acquired only through long apprenticeships. The women's bureau of the United States Department of Labor has rated the average woman's strength at 570/1,000 of a man's, which it was said, made it clear that women never would replace men in the jobs' involving heavy lifting.

However, some fifteen years later when my family was living in Troy, New York, with three kids, I welded a local farmer's plough shaft. To everyone's surprise, including my own, the shaft held.

From Receptionist to Payroll Unit Factory Worker

Jean Gates, California

I vividly remember hearing an announcement over the radio about Pearl Harbor being bombed by the Japanese on December 7th. My young brother and I were home alone, listening to the radio when the news came on. I can still feel the shock. The day following the attack, President Roosevelt announced we were at war with Japan. Another memory is being dumbfounded when the Japanese students were gone from my school. There was a lot of hysteria and possible sightings of Japanese submarines off the coast only made the situation worse. Barrage balloons began to be strategically placed around the harbor in Los Angeles and as I lay in bed I could hear craft fire.

I grew up in my birthplace of Fullerton, California, a part of Orange Country. It was an agricultural town with a population of 17,000. Situated between Fullerton and Brea, another small town, were great numbers of oil wells. Up until the Second World War, I lived a rather small town life. I did not concern myself with what was happening in the rest of the world. To me, a big deal was going shopping in Santa Ana, the county seat.

During 1942, an airbase was built in Santa Ana for basic training pilots. I read in the paper they needed civilian workers so I applied for my first job. I had taken business classes in school, earning myself enough credits by that point. I was hired. We wore name badges with our pictures on it and passed through security at the gate. It was exciting to be a part of the war effort. Employees worked six days a week and alternated holidays. Each day I rode to work with a man, his daughter, and two other girls. Later on, the man's son was killed in action. He was not able to talk about it, just handed me the telegram to read it.

My job was as a receptionist. The switchboard I manned was old-fashioned. For every call, I had to push a plug into a hole to connect the person calling and then pull it when the call was finished. My direct boss was a tough man and did not like the "ninety-day wonders." They were the men who came for basic training, but were not in the regular army. It was very common for my boss to yell, even at me, but I was not intimidated by it for some reason.

He had been at Pearl Harbor along with his master sergeant. It was there on the field of the attack that my boss had been promoted and while he was able to walk away from the war with this honor, soldiers staggered away with vivid memories of their best friends dying. Several servicemen were unable to deal with the anguish and the harsh reality of the war, ultimately committing suicide. Tragedies happened on and off the field, though. One day I was sitting at my desk when I heard a whining sound which abruptly stopped. The pilot had been killed during a routine training.

Dances at the base were a common activity for servicemen. A bus would pick the women up in town and bring us there. I loved to dance so I accepted the offer of anyone who asked. Once I even saw Billie Holiday at a Black night club on Central Avenue. I never lacked for dates and there were a few I especially liked, but it never went further than that. While the men and I did have a great deal of fun together, those were still tragic times of war. Many of them suffered from loneliness and during the holidays, I invited to my house those soldiers who had nowhere to go. They were apart from their families and truly appreciated everything offered to them.

I worked at the base for the entire duration of the war and advanced to several jobs. The hardest position was working for the payroll department. The job was strict on its accuracy and we were not allowed room for mistakes. Our work included taking the soldier's entire service record and going through it page by page to see what each man was owed. Toward the end of the war, we were getting American prisoners of war who had not been paid in quite some time. We had to pay close attention for promotions, decorations, anything that would mean more money, or money that would be lost because of demotions or demerits.

Toward the end of the war German and Italian prisoners of war were held on our base. They were made to take care of the maintenance and yard work and we were not allowed to fraternize with them. At that time, I had strong feelings against Germany and Japan so I did not look or speak to them. However, two girls were fired because they flirted with them.

My cousin was a navigator instructor stationed on the base where I worked for a short time. He also served as a navigator on bombers in the South Pacific. In 1947 he was still in the service. One mission was a B-29 flight, a maiden trip around the world. Sadly, the plane crashed into the Aegean Sea and nothing was ever recovered. I recall going home from work in Los Angeles and seeing his picture in the newspaper. This was the first my family knew of it, and the only loss we saw in the war.

The war changed people's lives and certainly did mine. I had always been rather shy and reserved and after the war, I felt that I grew up and came into my own. I no longer felt like a misfit. My introverted personality transformed into a more self-confident one and I knew from then on I would be able to take care of myself. In so many ways, Pearl Harbor became a major turning point in my life.

Aiding the War Effort, as a High School Student

Josephine Maupen, California

December 7, 1941 seems many light years past. A war in Hawaii was something that did not concern an immature 14-year-old girl from Tiltonsville, Ohio. I had never even heard of Pearl Harbor. We suffered many of the inconveniences the rest of the country did, such as gas and food rationing, but for a family that lived in a time where dinners were simple, fish was available, and large gardens and fruit trees were plentiful, it did not seem as though the war was touching our life.

Slowly, it encroached upon us. Eight of my cousins were either drafted or volunteered for the service. It was then that the war hit home. I figured it was the patriotic thing to do when I heard that the Air Force in Dayton, Ohio, was hiring for summer employment. I appealed to my father's sense of patriotism to allow me to apply. Reluctantly, he gave me permission.

On June 12, 1944, I was hired by the Army Air Force to go to Patterson Field in Dayton, Ohio, to work during the summer months. We left Wheeling, West Virginia, by bus and six hours later arrived in Fairfield, Ohio. We lived in a Quonset hut, but that was divided into rooms accommodating two people to each.

It was like a dream come true. Finally, I had left a town of 1,500 and was now near a big city, Dayton. We received our meals at the base and there were dances and activities to provide entertainment for us. We were able to come and go as we pleased and there was little or no supervision.

My first experience of a reality check was to see a B-29 brought into the field. The area where the tail gunner would have sat was riveted with bullet marks. It did not take long to realize that someone died when the plane was out.

From what I was told, our purpose for being there was because the war had already continued on for three years and there was a shortage of new planes. The old ones were, instead, returned to our field where we took them apart where possible and readied them to return to war. Every job varied, but none were more important than others. Some of the workers folded parachutes or repaired instruments and others worked with radiators. My main job was to wire a manifold or to add the spark plugs. For the most part, it was assembly line work. Each of us had only a small window of time to complete each task and we could only do the work that we could be trained quickly for.

There were many experiences I had, some funny, some sad. It was a period of life in which my friends and I grew up. When I returned home to finish school, our first casualty of the war hit our small community. Somehow, I felt that I had done a very small part in helping the war effort, and my work had done a big part in helping me mature into a responsible adult.

Single in Florida . . . Date at a POW Camp

Helen Rezendes, Florida

I was the second of twelve children, eight boys and four girls. Born in Thomas County, Georgia, on April 18, 1926, my siblings and I grew up on a farm. Even though it was during the Depression, I had a wonderful childhood. None of the children had a clue that we were poor. There was always plenty of food on the table for us.

In 1943, when I first graduated from high school, college was out of the question because there was not enough money in the family to send me away. I found a job in a branch of the Dale Mabry Air Force Base in Tallahassee. There at the Officer's Club I worked as a secretary. At night time, we would ride bicycles to the outskirts where there were big towers. Civilians were supposed to count any passing planes and call the Civil Defense with identification. The government wanted to be sure that they were American planes. Also around those moonlit hours, our town would have air raid drills.

A year later I went to live with my aunt and cousin in Panama City so that I could work at the Wainwright Shipyard. It was there that Liberty Ships were constructed. All three of us worked there. My cousin and I took on the graveyard shift from eleven P.M. until seven A.M. We were paid more for the shift. When war escalated there were times when we would work both days and nights. We never went home! It often got to the point that we were so exhausted we just had to sleep. I have no idea how many ships were made, but everyone was constantly busy and we frequently launched ships. My aunt's job was strikingly different from ours. She held the position of being the only female at the shipyard who drafted the prints of the electrical workings.

Around seven o'clock at night, my cousin and I would go to the USO where I was a Liberty Belle. It was a group of young women who entertained the GIs. On occasional afternoons, instead of going to dances, we would write letters for amputees or those who could not write for themselves. When we had a date, we always had to leave early to be sure we arrived at work on time. Our dates would usually be arranged between seven and ten o'clock. We would then catch a bus and rush off to work. The men we dated were sailors and soldiers. We were not allowed to date those men we met at the USO. There were strict rules we were expected to abide by.

At the Shipyard, my official job was a cost accountant. We used MacBee cards, which were a forerunner of computers. The cards had to go through a little machine and the names of employees were typed in. It would then print out things such as their Social Security number and their department to be cut out. Once this was finished, we would put the cards through the collators. Each one would be posted on a National Business Machine, which I operated. The noise was terrible. It sounded like I was in a factory with all the clatter going on nonstop. There were a number of these machines and a large amount of people working in the department.

Bond drives were held at work. From each department, the girl considered to be the most beautiful was selected to sell war bonds. The reason for it was that the prettier she looked, the more war bonds were bought in her name. In honor of this, lavish dances were held. The officers from Tyndall Air Force Base were invited to attend because they were the only men, besides the department heads at the Shipyard, who had money to spend. A lot of the personnel held high, well-paying jobs and they would go to these socials and purchase a war bond in order to dance with us. It was like *Gone with the Wind*.

I had one experience that was exciting. I met a Captain who was the commandant of a POW camp. It was far out in the woods and one day he said that he would pick me up early Sunday morning to attend. We would be gone all day. The trip there was long and I remember wondering if we would ever get to the camp. Finally, we arrived and pulled up alongside a tower. Men stood there with guns and barbed wire surrounded the area. It was incredibly frightening at first, but, actually, I had a wonderful time that day. We had delicious food cooked by German chefs and served by German POWs. I recall that they were neither allowed to look at any American woman that came in nor to say a word to anyone. They could not make an indication that we were anything other than another human being to them, but they were Prisoners of War . . . They were lucky to be alive!

In August of 1945, peace was declared and we all were handed our pink slips. Those of us at the Shipyard worked straight through September, trying to get everything packed up and ready for storage. Along with our productions, we packed away boxes of our suffering and fears of being at war, hoping to never re-open them.

A New Wave of Female Engineers

Jean Geelan, Florida

It was in Osceola, Wisconsin, that I was born in 1922. During my adolescent years, my father inherited numerous houses in Lakeland, Florida, and when his company went bankrupt during the Depression, we moved there. I went to FSCW and majored in business. I wanted to be an architect, but my father thought it was impractical for two reasons. First, I would have to go to Gainesville to study and they did not allow women in unless they were 21. Secondly, you had to have two years of general college previously. My father assumed even if I went, I would probably end up getting married early on and waste all that education. In the end, I only took two years at Florida State.

I was still in school when Pearl Harbor was bombed. It was a Sunday and I had taken the bus to an art show. It was on our way back that we were all made aware of what had happened. It was a complete shock. Everyone ran to help our country retaliate and it did cross my mind to join the Navy. Actually, that summer after my sophomore year, I took on a full-time job. I was employed by the United States Engineers to help build an airbase in Lakeland. They had called it Dranefield at the time, but it is now known as Lakeland Airport.

The Corps of Engineers had their regular office there. I served as a file clerk and the only other females employed were secretaries. The rest of the employees were civilian men. The boss of the outfit was the only man who was actually in the Army Corps, in uniform.

The airbase was five to ten miles away from my house and I would stand on the street corner and wait until someone picked me up. At that time, everyone shared rides to work. There was also a bus that we could take that went through the Air Corps camps nearby, but if we wanted to catch a ride, we had to be careful to pick it up on the way out, rather than on the ride in. The camp was still being built and there were no barracks, only tents to sleep in, nor were there indoor bathrooms. A large water tower opened up the sprinklers and the men would stand outside and shower publicly. In those days, seeing a man in that situation would be embarrassing, so we were always careful to avoid it.

At work, we had a small temporary office building they moved onto the property. It was set on bricks in the middle of the wilderness and there they built an airbase. There was no plumbing, only outhouses. Gradually, it began to build up and they brought in Army Air Corps to be stationed there. They started bringing in bombers and it was a staging field for groups going overseas. The women befriended many nice young men, and just like in the movies, waved good-bye to them when they went overseas.

While I was there, my father saw an article in *Newsweek* about the Curtiss-Wright cadettes. He knew I wanted to be an engineer and this sounded like an exciting way to become one. I responded to the article and asked to join the program. It had already been filled, but they took me anyway. For their program, they send nearly 2,000 girls to seven different universities. I had left a boyfriend up in Minnesota, so I asked if that was where I could be sent. Surprisingly, they agreed to my request, but instead of meeting my old boyfriend, I met my husband there.

A course on high altitude had been offered at the university. A new altitude chamber had been built and several of us volunteered for it because it sounded so interesting. Real male engineer students were there and my husband was one of them. There were no restrictions on dating other students and I found that being from Florida, I was a novelty girl.

Moving from Florida State to Minnesota was like going from alpha to omega. There possibly could have been 50,000 to 60,000 students, making it, at the time, the largest campus in the country. We all needed a map to get around and it was quite an adventure. There were almost no men, though, except for those in military training. All the fraternity houses had been emptied to move in army and naval training groups.

My training lasted ten months and I attended classes for forty hours a week. We had only male teachers and it took time for them to get used to a female class. Some of them were very shy in the beginning and often blushed when addressing us. One teacher absolutely cracked up during the first class, later on confessing to us that he had never before faced a room full of girls, of women.

It was a huge shock to the teachers. The women who were there were a choice bunch, having already taken two years or more of college math. They did not know how or what to teach us, so the men just taught us as much as possible. They were amazed at how much we managed to learn.

Our program was designed specifically for a Curtiss-Wright Airplane Factory in Columbus, Ohio. We were taught all the courses applying to the airframe that a graduate engineer would take. Our classes started out with fractions and numbers and went on through calculus. We completed courses in aerodynamics, in structures and stress analysis, as well as in engineering drafting. The women were even given a gym class and the option of taking bowling as a full-credited course. The women studied hard and soon, our ten-month period was completed. Proudly, we all walked away from the experience with three years of credit in the Engineering Department, given to us by the university.

There were few dropouts. Nearly 100 fledgling engineers (and Rudder) went on to Columbus, Ohio in December of that year and the majority worked there until the end of World War II—many advancing to full engineering positions and some to supervisory roles. At the war's end, the Curtiss-Wright Cadettes fanned out literally all over the world. Some continued in engineering, others entered entirely different fields, but few will forget or regret the unique adventure they shared.

An interesting sidelight: When I was assigned to the Structures Department at Curtiss Columbus, I was shocked to find I was listed as a "secretary." (One secretary and I were the only women in the department.) I really objected and finally earned the title of "junior stress analyst." That was the entering level for graduate engineers.

REFLECTIONS: YESTERDAY

In a perfect world everyone would be on the same page. In reality, even in wartime there is dissention over government procedure as in the ensuing years since the 9/11/01 attack. *America's Home Front Heroes* shows how great challenges during World War II brought people together!

In retrospect, the civilian population during World War II was probably unaware of the potential for enemy invasion of our country at any moment. Most were just regular Americans thrown together by circumstances into a mix of patriotism and naïveté, and the chemistry worked. It was a time when Americans collectively declared, "we can and will do our share from home to help battle-weary troops win the war."

There should be a permanent memorial specific to the home front heroes: shipbuilders, aircraft test pilots and mechanics, factory workers, farmers, nurses, doctors, and ordinary men, women, and children who served on the American home front in World War II. However, in March 2004, a new memorial in Washington, D.C., was justly dedicated to honor all our fighting heroes, and will serve as a reminder of their sacrifice.

Unexpected courage and strength is often the positive side of war. After the London, England, "blitz" which began on December 20, 1940, in which a total of 40,000 lives were lost as a result of bombing by the German Luftwaffe, a young artist at the time and witness to this massacre, was recently quoted as saying, "I don't understand the strength of people. The more the Germans hit us, the more we refused to submit." Enough said!

REFLECTIONS: TODAY

Remember how we felt immediately after the vicious attack on September 11, 2001? We were incensed by the terrorists' audacity, saddened by the loss of life and human dignity, helpless to retaliate within twenty-four hours but determined to go after them quickly, and afraid they would soon attack again.

Many young people responded by enlisting in the armed forces, but the civilian home front sat by with folded arms giving little consideration to how they could help in the war against terrorism. Let others decide who dropped the ball but Americans have proven in the past to be smart, resourceful, and determined. Despite disagreement and healthy debate on government policy surely civilians today could have a constructive role to play as their contribution to the on-going war. Thus far, we have yet to feel that strong connection between home front and the battlefronts that were felt during World War II.

Thanks to U.S. government vigilance a follow-up attack has thus far been avoided, leading to a certain amount of complacency. Sadly it seems that it would take another terrorist attack to motivate civilian response. However, certain lifestyle modifications are in place as air travelers now experience flight delays and must submit to body and baggage searches for possible weapons, and in some large cities there is now an ever-present display of armed guards. Will further modifications to our daily routine be imposed? Only time will tell. If pressed for comparisons to the World War II daily civilian sacrifice, one might say we are now experiencing little more than "an inconvenient home front."

We could write a new chapter in American history by focusing on the big picture in regard to the war effort. Just think, with a successful outcome history could recount the aftermath of September 11, 2001 as the beginning of the end of radical Islam's international terrorism. We must remember that the American home front is the bedrock of our democracy and our strength as citizens lies in our ability to unite in thought and deed.

INDEX

Note: Page numbers in *italics* denote illustrations.

Akielaszek, Stanley, *71*
Arthur, Jean, *68*

Barrett, Lucille, 23
Barzda, Justin, 75–76
Breise, Anne, 102–104
Brooklyn Navy Yard, 105
Brown, Gordon P., 39–43, *40–43*
Buffington, Helen Toles, xviii, 26–35
Burke, Mina, xxiii, 100–101

car sharing advertisement, 98
children, 16–18, 21–22
Closely Watched Trains (Barrett), 23
Cole-Beers, Anne, 79–81, *80*
college student, journal notes from, 26–35
Conscientious Objector, 56–58
Corsair aircraft, 77–78, *78*

death news, 9–12, *10*
Dempsey, Jack, 72–74, *73*
Denman, Joan, 62–66
DiBattista, Lee, 77–78
DiMaggio, Joe, xxi

draft, xviii, 29
duty, importance given to, 54–55

Economic Cooperation Administration (ECA), xxii
economy, post-World War II, xxi
emotions, during World War II, 13–15
European Recovery Program, xxii

female engineers, 115–117
female factory workers, *96–97*, 99, 100–109
Fonda, Henry, xxi
4-F, 59–61

Gable, Clark, xxi
gasoline stickers, xix, 98
Gates, Jean, 107–109
Geelan, Jean, 115–117
German immigrant, 36–38
Germany, xvii
G.I. Bill of Rights, xxiii
goodbye note, 23
Great Britain, xvii
Greenberg, Robert, xix, 7–8
Greist, E. Harold, Jr., 13–15

Hazelip, Charles, 16–18
high school student, 110–111
history, xvii
Hope, Bob, xx
Hopkins, Frank S., 91–93

Inniss, Clarence, 62–66
internment camps, an American's
    viewpoint, 52–53
Islam, xxii
Ivey, Mozzelle Bearden, 54–55

jail incident, during World War II, 7–8
Japanese Americans, 47, 48–51, 51,
    52–53
Japanese-American relocation sites,
    during World War II, 50
Jasper, Norman, 36–38

Kerker, Barton, 9–12, 11, 12
Kerker, Earl, 9–12
Key West, Florida (1941), 89–90
Kostyra, Eric, 71
Kostyra, Martha, 69–71, 70
Kowalsky, Mary, xix, 86–88

Leach, Douglas, xx
Lend-Lease Act, xvii
Leynes, Bernhardt, 19
Leynes, Lynette, 19–20, 20

McConnell, W.V., 59–61
McManus, Marion, 72–74, 73
Markoff, Del, xxi, 84–85
Marshall Plan, xxii
Maupen, Josephine, 110–111
MIAs, news about, 39–43
Miller, J. Howard, graphic by, 99
Motivalli, Margaret, 3–6, 6
Motivalli, Maurice, 5

National Catholic Community
    Service, xx
National Traders Aid Association, xx

National Jewish Welfare Aid
    Association, xx
Navy WAVE Pharmacist Mate,
    79–81
Newspaperman, 91–93
Nisei, 48–51

Organization for European Economic
    Cooperation (OEEC), xxii

Pearl Harbor bombing, 46; civilian
    survivor, 3–6, 5, 6
Pershing, John J., 14
Phifer, Gregg, 56–58
Pollack, Ida, 105–106
postwar period, xxi, 84–85
prisoners of war, 112–114

Reflections, 119, 121
Rezendes, Helen, 112–114
riot, 62–66
Roosevelt, Franklin, xxiii, xxiv, 14
Rosie the Riveter, xx, 99

Salvation Army, xx
Schmidt, John E., Jr., 21–22
September 11, 2001 attack, xxii
Serviceman's Readjustment Act, xxiii
shortages, xix
The Stage Door Canteen, xx
Stewart, Martha, 69, 70, 71
Stewart, James, xxi

Takahashi, Gene, 48–51
Truman, Harry, xxiv, 18
Tullo, William L., 68

United Service Organizations
    (USO), xx
USO Volunteer, 82–83

van Allen, Vivian, 82–83
V-Mails, xx

war on terror, xxiii
wartime housewife/mother, 69–71
Webster, Terri, *1*, 25–26
White, Armer, 89–90
Williams, Mary E., 52–53
Williams, Ted, xxi

Women's Army Auxiliary Corps,
   104
working together, 86–88

Young Men's Christian Association,
   xx

About the Author

STACY ENYEART is a freelance portrait writer and former newspaper film critic, advertising copywriter, magazine publisher/editor, and film documentary script writer. An inherent curiosity about people from all walks of life have inspired her ro put pen to paper regarding their life experiences. Prime examples are the home front heroes in this book.

Currently she serves a board member of the National League of American Pen Women (Fairfield County branch), as well as the Connecticut Press Club. She is also a recent recipient of the Community Service Award from AARP headquarters in Washington, D.C.